Reprinted 1993
© 1991 Coombe Books
All rights reserved
ISBN 0 86283 411 2
Printed and bound in Singapore

WOK
COOKING
COOMBE BOOKS

Contents

Introduction
page 4

Soups and Starters
pages 6–14

Fish and Seafood
pages 15–21

Meat Dishes
pages 22–42

Meals with Poultry
pages 43–51

Vegetables, Chutney and Sauces
pages 52–59

Sweets
pages 60–61

Glossary
pages 62–63

Index
page 64

Introduction

The wok is an ancient Chinese cooking utensil known for its versatility. It can be used for stir-frying, deep frying, steaming, boiling and braising a wide variety of food.

Stir-Fried Leeks and Lamb (above), Beef and Oyster Sauce (above right) and Pork with Plum Sauce (right).

The traditional wok is made of heavy gauge carbon steel which conducts heat well, giving a quick high temperature. However, this medium will rust if not oiled and given proper care. Lengthy cooking in liquid may impart a metallic taste to the food or may cause the discolouration of white liquids or food. Aluminium and stainless steel woks are also available and are a good choice, particularly if steaming, braising, boiling, or cooking for a long time. These woks need no seasoning but do not heat as efficiently as carbon steel.

Cooking times in this book are only a guide, as actual times will vary with the kind of wok you use and the intensity of the heat source.

There are three types of wok: round-bottomed, for use on gas burners – with the use of a ring-base for stability; flat bottomed, for electric ranges; and electric woks, which can be used to cook at the table or anywhere there is a power point. Other equipment that may be needed includes a curved, long-handled spatula, and curved slotted spoon (which fit into the curved shape of the wok), a domed lid, a metal trivet or bamboo steamer and a deep fat frying thermometer.

Stir-frying, a fuel and timesaver. It is unique to wok cooking, where small pieces of food are toss-cooked in minutes over intense heat, in a very small amount of oil. The shape of the wok allows for tossing with abandon. Food is cooked in a matter of minutes and the flavours and juices are sealed in, resulting in succulent meat, poultry and seafood, and tender and crisp vegetables. Nutritional values are retained, as are the fresh and bright colours of vegetables.

A number of steps followed will lead to ease of cooking and best results:

☆ Heat wok before adding oil.

☆ Have all ingredients needed for the recipe prepared and to hand before beginning to cook. Care should be taken in the preparation of the food so that everything cooks in a short time and adds to the appearance of the final dish.

☆ Any sauces or seasonings should generally be prepared in advance.

☆ Slice meat and poultry very thinly and evenly (it will slice easier if partially frozen and a very sharp knife is used).

☆ Ingredients that take the longest to cook should be put into the wok first.

☆ Add a small amount of food at a time – in batches if necessary.

☆ Ensure everything is ready for serving, including family or guests, as the food must be eaten immediately it is cooked. It is not the sort of cooking that can be done ahead of time.

Deep frying. Points to note when cooking with oil:

☆ Care must be taken not to move or tilt the wok when it contains hot oil.

☆ Ensure wok is uncovered when heating oil.

☆ Ensure handles are not sticking over edge of stove.

☆ Be careful if adding moist food as it tends to spatter.

☆ After cooking, allow oil to cool before pouring out or returning to its container.

Steaming and Braising. Points to note when steaming and braising:

☆ During cooking some steam will condense and form drops of water under the domed lid. To shield the food, cover with a piece of greaseproof paper.

☆ Check the water level once in a while and top up as needed.

A few well-chosen ingredients, now readily available, will give you the authentic flavours for many a delicious Oriental dish, enabling you to savour the pleasures of exotic Eastern cuisine.

Though the wok is primarily an Oriental utensil, I have interspersed the Eastern dishes with a variety of Western-style recipes, since wok cooking adapts well to many types of cuisine.

Soups and Starters

Wonton Soup

PREPARATION TIME: 15 minutes

COOKING TIME: 15 minutes

SERVES: 4 people

225g (8oz) minced pork
4 spring onions, chopped finely
½ tsp finely chopped root ginger
15ml (1 tbsp) light soy sauce
115g (4oz) wonton wrappers
1 tsp cornflour
5ml (1 tsp) sesame oil
5ml (1 tsp) Chinese wine, or dry
*   sherry*
1 tsp sugar
Salt
Pepper
1 litre (2 pints) chicken stock
2.5ml (½ tsp) sesame oil

Garnish
Coriander, or finely chopped spring
*   onion*

Place in a bowl the minced pork, spring onions, ginger, soy sauce, 5ml (1 tsp) sesame oil, Chinese wine, sugar, cornflour, salt and pepper. Mix together well and set aside. Heat stock in wok and bring to the boil. Season with salt and pepper. Wrap ½ teaspoon of pork mixture into each wonton wrapper. Close tightly and drop into stock. Cook for 5 minutes. Wontons will usually rise to the surface when cooked. Add 2.5ml (½ tsp) sesame oil and stir in. Garnish with spring onion or fresh coriander. Serve hot.

Chinese Combination Soup

PREPARATION TIME: 30 minutes

COOKING TIME: 20 minutes

SERVES: 4 people

4 dried Chinese mushrooms
225g (8oz) chicken
115g (4oz) fine/thread egg noodles
1 clove garlic, sliced thinly
1 tsp finely sliced root ginger
¼ small cabbage, shredded
600ml (1 pint) chicken stock
15ml (1 tbsp) peanut oil
2 eggs, beaten
15ml (1 tbsp) dark soy sauce
15ml (1 tbsp) sherry

15ml (1 tbsp) water
1 tsp cornflour
2 shallots, peeled and sliced finely

Soak mushrooms in hot water for 20 minutes. Remove and discard stems. Slice mushroom caps thinly. Soak noodles in boiling salted water for 2 minutes. Rinse in cold water. Drain. Slice chicken finely. Heat wok and add peanut oil. Add garlic and ginger, and fry gently for 5 minutes, then discard. Add chicken, and fry for a few minutes until meat has turned white. Add mushrooms, shallots, cabbage and stock. Bring to the boil and simmer for 5 minutes. Gradually pour in eggs and stir so that they cook in shreds. Mix cornflour with 15ml (1 tbsp) of water, and pour into soup, stirring continuously. Cook for 2 minutes or until soup thickens. Add noodles, soy sauce and sherry. Serve immediately.

This page: Wonton Soup (top) and Curry Soup with Meatballs (bottom).

Facing page: Chinese Combination Soup (top) and Eggflower Soup (bottom).

Curry Soup with Meatballs

PREPARATION TIME:	30 minutes
COOKING TIME:	20 minutes
SERVES:	4 people

Meatballs
225g (8oz) lean minced beef
1 clove garlic, crushed
1 onion, peeled and chopped finely
½ tsp salt
½ tsp curry powder, or ¼ tsp curry paste
½ tsp ground cinnamon
½ tsp ground cloves
½ tsp ground pepper
30g (1oz) breadcrumbs
1 small egg, lightly beaten

Broth
1 tsp garam masala
1 tsp turmeric
600ml (1 pint) water
1 clove garlic, crushed
1 onion, peeled and finely chopped
1 tsp curry leaves
½ cup desiccated coconut, soaked in 1 cup hot water for 15 minutes
30ml (2 tbsps) peanut oil

Mix together meatball ingredients, and form into small balls about the size of walnuts. Heat wok, add oil and, when hot, fry meatballs. When browned well all over, remove with a slotted spoon, and drain on absorbent paper. Carefully drain oil from wok. Add 5ml (1 tsp) of oil, and fry spices for 30 seconds. Add onion, curry leaves, and garlic, and cook together for 3 minutes. Meanwhile, strain coconut in a sieve, press out as much liquid as possible, and discard the pulp. Add water and coconut milk to the wok and simmer together for 5 minutes. Adjust seasoning. Strain soup and return to wok. Add meatballs and simmer a further 5 minutes. Serve hot.

Hot and Sour Soup

PREPARATION TIME:	30 minutes
COOKING TIME:	30 minutes
SERVES:	4 people

115g (4oz) lean pork fillet
4 dried Chinese mushrooms
60g (2oz) bamboo shoots, sliced
1 square beancurd, diced
30ml (2 tbsps) sunflower or vegetable oil
1 litre (2 pints) light, clear stock, or hot water plus 2 chicken stock cubes
1 tsp cornflour
30ml (2 tbsps) cold water
5ml (1 tsp) sesame oil

Marinade
15ml (1 tbsp) light soy sauce
45ml (3 tbsps) brown vinegar
30ml (2 tbsps) water
5ml (1 tsp) sesame oil
Salt
Pepper

Garnish
Fresh coriander

Soak Chinese mushrooms for 20 minutes in hot water. Meanwhile, slice pork into thin slivers. Make the marinade by combining light soy sauce, brown vinegar, water, sesame oil, and salt and pepper. Pour over pork and leave for 30 minutes. Drain mushrooms. Remove and discard stalks. Slice caps very finely. Remove pork from marinade, and reserve marinade. Heat wok, and add sunflower or vegetable oil. When hot, stir-fry pork, mushrooms and bamboo shoots for 2 minutes. Add stock and bring to the boil. Simmer for 10 minutes. Add beancurd, marinade, and salt and pepper to taste. Slake cornflour in 30ml (2 tbsps) of cold water. Add to soup and allow to simmer for 5 minutes. Add sesame oil and sprinkle with fresh coriander. Serve hot.

Chicken and Asparagus Soup

PREPARATION TIME:	10 minutes
COOKING TIME:	45 minutes

SERVES: 4 people

450g (1lb) chicken pieces
1 onion, peeled and chopped roughly
1 carrot, chopped roughly
1 stick celery, chopped roughly
4 peppercorns
300g (10oz) can asparagus pieces
1 litre (2 pints) water
Salt
Pepper

Garnish
Chopped parsley

Remove chicken meat from bones and cut into fine shreds. Put chicken bones, onion, carrot, celery, peppercorns and water in wok, and season with salt and pepper. Bring to the boil, reduce heat, and simmer for 30 minutes. Strain and return stock to wok. Add chicken shreds, and simmer until chicken is cooked. Add undrained asparagus pieces. Adjust seasoning. Serve sprinkled with chopped parsley.

Eggflower Soup

PREPARATION TIME:	10 minutes
COOKING TIME:	10 minutes
SERVES:	4 people

600ml (1 pint) chicken stock
2 eggs, lightly beaten
15ml (1 tbsp) light soy sauce
400g (14oz) can plum tomatoes
2 spring onions, chopped finely

Drain and chop tomatoes, removing pips, and reserve juice. Bring soy sauce, tomato juice and stock to the boil in the wok. Add tomatoes and half the spring onions, and cook for 2 minutes. Dribble beaten eggs in gradually, stirring continuously. Serve immediately, sprinkled with remaining spring onions.

Chicken and Asparagus Soup (below) and Hot and Sour Soup (right).

cooking. Use a slotted spoon to remove, and drain on absorbent paper. If necessary, store in an airtight container until needed.

Chicken Liver Pâté

PREPARATION TIME: 20 minutes

COOKING TIME: 20 minutes

SERVES: 4 people as a starter

225g (8oz) chicken livers, trimmed
115g (4oz) butter
1 medium onion, peeled and chopped
*   finely*
1 bay leaf
1 clove garlic, crushed
15ml (1 tbsp) brandy
5ml (1 tsp) Worcestershire sauce
Salt
Pepper

Garnish
Sprig of parsley

Heat wok and add half of the butter. Add onion, garlic and bay leaf, and fry gently until onion is soft but not coloured. Increase heat, and add chicken livers and salt and freshly-ground black pepper to taste, and fry for 5 minutes, turning regularly. Add Worcestershire sauce and stir well. Remove from heat, and set aside to cool. Meanwhile, cream remaining butter. Remove bay leaf and chop liver finely – this can be done in a blender. Push through a sieve; beat in creamed butter and stir in brandy. Fill into individual ramekin dishes or into a china dish. If keeping, smooth over surface and cover with clarified butter. Garnish with a sprig of parsley.

Cheese Nibbles

PREPARATION TIME: 20 minutes

COOKING TIME: 20 minutes

MAKES: 40 pieces

60g (2oz) Gruyère cheese
60g (2oz) Emmenthal cheese
1 egg, lightly beaten
30ml (2 tbsps) milk
1 tsp dry English mustard
1 clove garlic, crushed

This page: Prawn Crisps/ Crackers (top left), Fried Bananas (centre right) and Poppadums (bottom).

Facing page: Chicken Liver Pâté (top) and Cheese Nibbles (bottom).

Poppadums

COOKING TIME: 5 minutes

Poppadums
Oil for deep frying

Heat oil in wok. When oil is hot, deep fry 1 poppadum at a time for 2-3 seconds, holding edges apart with forks. They will puff up, and should be pale golden in colour. If browning, reduce heat of oil. If not cooking quickly enough, increase heat. Remove, shaking off excess oil, and drain on absorbent paper. They may be eaten straight away, or when cool may be kept in an airtight container until needed.

Fried Bananas

PREPARATION TIME: 5 minutes

COOKING TIME: 10 minutes

SERVES: 4 people

3-4 bananas
15ml (1 tbsp) lemon juice
30ml (2 tbsps) oil
Salt

Peel bananas and slice diagonally. Heat wok and add oil. When hot, add bananas. Fry, turning carefully until browned well all over. Sprinkle with lemon juice and a pinch of salt, and serve as an accompaniment to a curry.

Prawn Crisps/Crackers (Krupuk)

COOKING TIME: 5 minutes

Prawn Crisps
Oil for deep frying

Heat oil in wok, and make sure the oil is hot, but not too hot. It should be hot enough to puff the prawn crisps in 2-3 seconds: if they brown, the oil is too hot. If it is not hot enough, they will take too long to cook, and will be tough and chewy. A few can be fried together, but do not put too many in as they need to be removed quickly before over-

Seafood Hot and Sour Soup

PREPARATION TIME: 20 minutes

COOKING TIME: 20 minutes

SERVES: 4 people

2 dried Chinese mushrooms
1 cake fresh beancurd, diced
115g (4oz) prawns or shrimps, shelled and de-veined
600ml (1 pint) light stock, preferably fish stock
60g (2oz) crab meat, or 2 crab-sticks, cut into 1.5cm (½") slices
1 tbsp oyster sauce
15ml (1 tbsp) light soy sauce
15ml (1 tbsp) lemon juice
½ tsp lemon rind, cut into slivers
15ml (1 tbsp) vegetable oil
1 red chilli, seeds removed, and finely sliced
2 spring onions, sliced
Salt
Pepper
5ml (1 tsp) sesame oil

Garnish
Fresh coriander, if desired

Soak mushrooms in hot water and set aside for 20 minutes. Heat wok, add vegetable oil and, when hot, stir-fry prawns, chilli, lemon rind and spring onions. Add stock, oyster sauce and light soy sauce, and bring to the boil. Reduce heat and simmer for 5 minutes. Add salt and pepper to taste. Remove hard stalks from mushrooms and slice caps finely. Add crab meat, beancurd and Chinese mushrooms to wok, and cook a further 5 minutes. Stir in lemon juice and sesame oil. Adjust seasoning, and serve sprinkled with fresh coriander leaves if desired.

Spring Rolls

PREPARATION TIME: 20 minutes

COOKING TIME: 30 minutes

MAKES: 12 rolls

225g (8oz) finely minced pork
1 red chilli, seeds removed, and sliced finely
10 canned water chestnuts, chopped
1 onion, peeled and chopped finely
1 clove garlic, crushed
½ tsp grated root ginger
1 tsp ground turmeric
30ml (2 tbsps) peanut oil
12 spring roll wrappers
Salt
Pepper
Peanut or vegetable oil for deep frying

Heat wok, add 30ml (2 tbsps) of peanut oil, and fry garlic, ginger,

30g (1oz) plain flour
1 tsp baking powder
Salt
Pepper
10 slices stale brown bread
Oil for deep frying

Sift together flour, baking powder,

mustard, and a pinch of salt and pepper. Grate cheese. Mix together cheese, egg, milk, garlic and flour mixture. Beat together well. Trim off bread-crusts, and cut each slice diagonally into 4 triangles. Spread one heaped teaspoon of mixture on each triangle of bread to cover well.

Heat oil in wok. When hot, carefully fry in batches with bread side up first. Deep fry until golden brown on both sides. Remove and drain on absorbent paper. Keep hot until all frying is completed. Serve hot.

13

Facing page: Seafood Hot
and Sour Soup (top) and
Sweetcorn and Chicken
Soup (bottom).

This page: Prawn Toast (top)
and Spring Rolls (right).

ground turmeric and onion for 3 minutes. Add pork, and stir-fry until pork is browning. Add water chestnuts and chilli, and salt and pepper to taste, and fry for a further 2 minutes. Remove from wok, and set aside to cool. Place spring roll wrapper with one corner pointing towards you. Spoon some of the mixture just in front of the centre. Fold over the corner nearest to you, and roll to centre. Fold the two side points into the centre and finish rolling up. They may be sealed with a paste of water and flour if necessary. Refrigerate until needed. Heat oil for deep frying in wok, and deep fry spring rolls in batches just before needed. Drain on absorbent paper, and serve warm with chilli or sweet-and-sour sauce.

Prawn Toast

PREPARATION TIME: 15 minutes

COOKING TIME: 15 minutes

MAKES: approximately 20 pieces

225g (8oz) prawns or shrimps, shelled and de-veined, and chopped finely
1 small egg, beaten
10ml (2 tsps) sherry
2 tsps oyster sauce
½ tsp grated root ginger
2 tsp cornflour
Salt
5 slices white bread
Oil for deep frying

Combine prawns, beaten egg, sherry, oyster sauce, grated ginger, cornflour and a pinch of salt. Using a 4cm (1½") round pastry cutter, cut out circles of bread. Spread mixture on each piece of bread to cover well. Heat oil in wok for deep frying. Fry in batches with bread side up first, until bread is golden brown. Remove and drain on absorbent paper. Keep hot until all frying is completed.

Sweetcorn and Chicken Soup

PREPARATION TIME: 15 minutes

COOKING TIME: 45 minutes

SERVES: 4 people

1 chicken, with giblets
225g (8oz) can creamy sweetcorn
1 onion, peeled and chopped roughly
1 carrot, scraped and chopped roughly

1 stick celery, chopped
6 peppercorns
Parsley stalks
1 bay leaf
1 litre (2 pints) water
Salt
Pepper

Garnish
Chopped parsley or chives

Clean chicken, and cut into quarters. Put into wok with giblets, chopped vegetables, peppercorns, bay leaf, parsley stalks, seasoning and water. Bring to the boil. Reduce heat and simmer for 30 minutes. Strain and return stock to wok. Remove meat from chicken and cut into fine shreds. Add undrained sweetcorn to stock, and bring to boil. Simmer for 5 minutes. Add chicken and cook for 1 minute. Sprinkle with chopped parsley or chives. Serve hot.

Rice Paper Prawn Parcels

PREPARATION TIME: 15 minutes

COOKING TIME: 15 minutes

MAKES: about 20 parcels

225g (8oz) prawns or shrimps, shelled and de-veined
6 spring onions, sliced finely
1 packet rice paper
1 egg white
½ tsp cornflour
150ml (¼ pint) peanut oil
5ml (1 tsp) Chinese wine, or 10ml (2 tsps) dry sherry
5ml (1 tsp) light soy sauce
1 tsp sugar
Salt
Pepper

Dry prepared prawns on absorbent paper. Mix egg white, cornflour, wine, sugar, soy sauce, spring

onions and seasoning together. Mix in prawns. Heat peanut oil in wok until hot. Wrap five or six prawns in each piece of rice paper. Gently drop in rice paper parcels and deep fry for about 5 minutes. Serve hot.

Crab Rolls

PREPARATION TIME: 20 minutes

COOKING TIME: 20 minutes

MAKES: 12 rolls

175g (6oz) crab meat, fresh or canned
3 spring onions, finely sliced
12 spring roll wrappers
30g (1oz) cellophane noodles
¼ tsp grated root ginger
1 tsp oyster sauce
2 tbsps finely chopped bamboo shoots
Salt
Vegetable or peanut oil for deep frying

Soak cellophane noodles in hot water for 8 minutes, or as directed, and drain. Flake crab meat, and drain if necessary. Combine crab meat with spring onions, noodles, ginger, bamboo shoots, oyster sauce, and salt to taste. Place spring roll wrappers with one corner pointing towards you. Spoon some of the mixture just before the centre. Fold over the corner nearest you and roll to centre. Fold the two side points into the centre, and roll up completely. They may be sealed with a paste of flour and water if necessary. Refrigerate until needed. Heat oil in wok and deep fry batches of spring rolls just before serving. Drain on absorbent paper. Serve warm with ginger sauce or sweet-and-sour sauce.

This page: **Crab Rolls (top) and Rice Paper Prawn Parcels (bottom).**

Facing page: **Ginger Scallops in Oyster Sauce (top) and Crispy Fish with Chilli (bottom).**

Fish and Seafood

Crispy Fish with Chilli

PREPARATION TIME: 40 minutes
COOKING TIME: 30 minutes
SERVES: 4 people

450g (1lb) fish fillets, skinned, bones removed, and cut into 2.5cm (1") cubes

Batter
60g (2oz) plain flour
1 egg, separated
15ml (1 tbsp) oil
75ml (5 tbsps) milk
Salt

Sauce
1 tsp grated root ginger
¼ tsp chilli powder
2 tbsps tomato purée
2 tbsps tomato chutney
30ml (2 tbsps) dark soy sauce
30ml (2 tbsps) Chinese wine or dry sherry
30ml (2 tbsps) water
1 tsp sugar
1 red chilli, seeds removed, and sliced finely
1 clove garlic, crushed
Salt
Pepper
Oil for deep frying

Sift the flour with a pinch of salt. Make a well in the centre, and drop in the egg yolk and oil. Mix to a smooth batter with the milk, gradually incorporating the flour. Beat well. Cover and set aside in a cool place for 30 minutes. Whisk egg white until stiff, and fold into batter just before using. Heat oil in wok. Dip fish pieces into batter and coat completely. When oil is hot, carefully lower fish pieces in and cook until cooked through and golden brown – about 10 minutes. Remove with a slotted spoon. Reheat oil and refry each fish piece for 2 minutes. Remove with a slotted spoon and drain on absorbent paper. Carefully remove all but 15ml (1 tbsp) of oil from wok. Heat oil, and add chilli, ginger, garlic, chilli powder, tomato purée, tomato chutney, soy sauce, sugar, wine and water, and salt and pepper to taste. Stir well over heat for 3 minutes. Increase heat and toss in fish pieces. Coat with sauce and, when heated through, serve immediately.

continuously. Return squid and cook until heated through. Place in a warm serving dish and serve hot with rice.

Ginger Scallops in Oyster Sauce

PREPARATION TIME: 10 minutes
COOKING TIME: 15 minutes
SERVES: 4 people

450g (1lb) scallops, cleaned, dried on
   absorbent paper, and sliced
10 spring onions, sliced diagonally
   into 2.5cm (1") slices
2.5cm (1") green ginger, peeled and
   sliced very thinly
Salt
30ml (2 tbsps) vegetable oil

Sauce
1 tbsp oyster sauce
15ml (1 tbsp) light soy sauce
2.5ml (½ tsp) sesame oil
1 tsp grated root ginger
1 tsp cornflour
75ml (5 tbsps) light stock, or 75ml
   (5 tbsps) hot water and half a
   chicken stock cube
Pinch of sugar

Combine oyster sauce, soy sauce, sesame oil, cornflour, sugar and grated ginger and set aside. Sprinkle the scallops with a pinch of salt. Heat wok, and add oil. Add sliced ginger and spring onions, and stir-fry gently for 1 minute. Raise heat to high. Add scallops and stir-fry for 1 minute. Add sauce mixture and stir in. Remove from heat, and stir in stock gradually. Return to heat and bring to the boil, stirring continuously. Simmer gently for 3 minutes, until sauce is slightly thickened. Adjust seasoning. Serve immediately with boiled rice.

Steamed Fish with Black Beans

PREPARATION TIME: 15 minutes
COOKING TIME: 15 minutes
SERVES: 4 people

1kg (2lbs) whole snapper, bass or
   bream, cleaned and scaled
1 tbsp salted black beans
2 cloves garlic, crushed
15ml (1 tbsp) light soy sauce
5ml (1 tsp) Chinese wine, or 10ml
   (2 tsps) dry sherry
1 tsp sugar
½ tsp cornflour
5ml (1 tsp) sesame oil
½ can bamboo shoots, cut into shreds
Salt
Pepper

Squid with Broccoli and Cauliflower

PREPARATION TIME: 15 minutes
COOKING TIME: 20 minutes
SERVES: 4 people

450g (1lb) squid, cleaned
1 onion, peeled and chopped roughly
225g (8oz) fresh broccoli florets
225g (8oz) fresh cauliflower florets
2 sticks celery, sliced diagonally
½ tsp grated root ginger
1 tbsp cornflour

30ml (2 tbsps) water
30ml (2 tbsps) light soy sauce
30ml (2 tbsps) Chinese wine, or dry
   sherry
2 tbsps oyster sauce
2.5ml (½ tsp) sesame oil
½ tsp sugar
150ml (¼ pint) oil, for deep frying
Salt
Pepper

Cut cleaned squid lengthways down centre. Flatten out with inside uppermost. With a sharp knife make a lattice design, cutting deep into squid flesh (to tenderise and make squid curl when cooking). Heat oil in wok. Add squid and cook until it curls. Remove from pan and drain on absorbent paper. Carefully pour off all but 15ml (1 tbsp) of oil. Add onion, celery, broccoli, cauliflower and ginger, and stir-fry for 3 minutes. Slake cornflour with water, and add soy sauce, wine, oyster sauce, sesame oil, sugar, and salt and pepper to taste. Mix well and add to wok. Bring to the boil and simmer for 3 minutes, stirring

Facing page: Squid with Broccoli and Cauliflower.

This page: Singapore Fried Noodles (below) and Steamed Fish with Black Beans (bottom).

Wash and clean fish well and dry with absorbent paper. Make 3 or 4 diagonal cuts in flesh of fish on each side. Rub garlic into cuts and place fish on a heat-proof dish. Rinse black beans in cold water, then crush with the back of a spoon. Add cornflour, sesame oil, soy sauce, sugar and wine, and salt and pepper and mix together well. Pour over fish. Sprinkle bamboo shoots on top of fish. Put plate on top of a bamboo steamer or metal trivet standing in wok. Add water, ensuring the level is below the level of the plate. Cover and bring to the boil. Steam for about 10 minutes after boiling point is reached. Ensure that the fish is cooked, but do not oversteam. Serve hot.

Stir-Fried Prawns and Mangetout

PREPARATION TIME: 5 minutes

COOKING TIME: 5 minutes

SERVES: 4 people

225g (8oz) prawns or shrimps, shelled and de-veined
115g (4oz) mangetout, trimmed
60ml (4 tbsps) peanut oil
30ml (2 tbsps) dry white wine
Juice of half a lemon
15ml (1 tbsp) light soy sauce
Pinch of salt
Black pepper

Garnish
Parsley

Blanch mangetout in boiling salted water for 1 minute. Drain and set aside. Heat wok, add the peanut oil, and stir-fry prawns for 30 seconds. Add mangetout, dry white wine, lemon juice, soy sauce, and salt and pepper, and toss together until heated through. Adjust seasoning and garnish with parsley. Serve immediately with boiled rice.

Seafood Combination

PREPARATION TIME: 20 minutes

COOKING TIME: 20 minutes

SERVES: 4 people

225g (8oz) prawns or shrimps, shelled and de-veined
115g (4oz) squid, cleaned, cut into 2.5cm (1") rings, opened up, and scored with lattice design
115g (4oz) mangetout, trimmed
115g (4oz) white fish fillets, cut into 2.5cm (1") cubes

1 stick celery, sliced diagonally
1 carrot, scraped and cut into matchstick strips
1 tsp grated root ginger
½ tsp salt
15ml (1 tbsp) dry white wine
1 egg white
1 tsp cornflour
Oil for deep frying

Combine wine, salt, egg white, grated ginger and cornflour, and mix well. Add prawns and fish, and toss well. Drain prawns and fish, reserving sauce. Blanch mangetout in boiling water for 1 minute. Drain. Heat oil in wok. Deep fry prawns, fish and squid for 2 minutes. Remove from pan and drain on

This page: Seafood Combination.

Facing page: Mediterranean Fish Stew (top) and Stir-Fried Prawns and Mangetout (bottom).

absorbent paper. Carefully remove oil from wok, reserving 15ml (1 tbsp) of oil in wok. Heat oil. Stir-fry carrot and celery for 3 minutes. Add mangetout and stir-fry a further 3 minutes. Add any remaining sauce and stir. Add seafood and toss well until heated through.

Honey Sesame Prawns

PREPARATION TIME: 20 minutes
COOKING TIME: 20 minutes
SERVES: 4 people

450g (1lb) prawns or shrimps, shelled and de-veined
2 tbsps cornflour
115g (4oz) self-raising flour
1 egg, lightly beaten
Pinch of salt
Pepper
150ml (¼ pint) water
Oil for deep frying
2 tbsps honey
1 tbsp sesame seeds
15ml (1 tbsp) sesame oil

Sift flour and salt and pepper into a bowl. Make a well in the centre and add egg and water, gradually bringing in the flour. Beat to a smooth batter and set aside for 10 minutes. Meanwhile, toss prawns in cornflour and coat well. Shake off any excess cornflour. Add prawns to batter and coat well. Heat oil in wok, and add prawns, a few at a time. Cook until batter is golden. Remove and drain on absorbent paper, and keep warm. Repeat until all prawns have been fried. Carefully remove hot oil from wok. Gently heat sesame oil in pan. Add honey and stir until mixed well and heated through. Add prawns to mixture and toss well. Sprinkle over sesame seeds and again toss well. Serve immediately.

Steamed Fish in Ginger

PREPARATION TIME: 20 minutes
COOKING TIME: 15 minutes
SERVES: 4 people

1.5kg (3lbs) whole snapper, bass or bream, cleaned and scaled

Stuffing
½ cup cooked rice
1 tsp grated root ginger
3 spring onions, sliced finely
10ml (2 tsps) light soy sauce
6 spring onions, cut into 5cm (2") lengths, then into fine shreds
3 pieces green ginger, cut into fine shreds

Garnish
Lemon slices and parsley, if desired

Mix together rice, grated ginger, sliced spring onion and soy sauce. Stuff rice mixture into cleaned fish cavity, packing in well. Place fish on a heat-proof plate, and arrange strips of spring onion and green ginger on top of fish. Put the plate on top of a bamboo steamer or metal trivet standing in wok. Add water, ensuring the water level is not up to the plate. Cover and bring to the boil. Steam for 10 minutes from boiling point. Ensure that the fish is cooked, but be sure not to oversteam the fish. Serve hot, garnished with lemon slices and parsley, if desired.

Singapore Fried Noodles

PREPARATION TIME: 20 minutes
COOKING TIME: 25 minutes
SERVES: 4 people

225g (8oz) packet egg noodles
225g (8oz) prawns or shrimps, shelled and de-veined
1 chicken breast, cut into shreds
115g (4oz) bean sprouts
2 cloves garlic, crushed
3 sticks celery, sliced diagonally
2 spring onions, sliced
1 red chilli, seeds removed, and sliced
1 green chilli, seeds removed, and sliced
1 tsp chilli powder
2 eggs, lightly beaten
45ml (3 tbsps) oil
Salt
Pepper

Garnish
Chilli flowers (carefully cut end of chilli into shreds, and soak in cold water until flower opens)

Soak noodles in boiling water for 8 minutes, or as directed. Drain noodles on absorbent paper and leave to dry. Heat wok, and add 15ml (1 tbsp) of oil. Add lightly beaten eggs, and salt and pepper to taste. Stir gently and cook until set. Remove from wok, and cut into thin strips and keep warm. Add remaining oil to wok. When hot, add garlic and chilli powder and fry for 30 seconds. Add chicken, celery, spring onions and red and green chillies, and stir-fry for 8 minutes or until chicken has cooked through. Add noodles, prawns and bean sprouts, and toss until well mixed and heated through. Serve with scrambled egg strips on top and garnish with chilli flowers.

Mediterranean Fish Stew

PREPARATION TIME: 20 minutes
COOKING TIME: 30 minutes
SERVES: 4 people

450g (1lb) white fish fillets, cut into 5cm (2") cubes
30ml (2 tbsps) olive oil
2 cloves garlic, crushed
1 onion, peeled and sliced finely
2 sticks celery, sliced
1 tbsp chopped parsley
1 tsp oregano
2 tbsps tomato purée
150ml (¼ pint) fish stock or water
30ml (2 tbsps) sweet Italian vermouth, or sweet sherry
115g (4oz) squid (optional), cleaned
2 leeks, white parts sliced finely
400g (14oz) can plum tomatoes
115g (4oz) flat mushrooms, sliced
Salt
Pepper

Garnish
Lemon slices
Parsley

Heat wok, and add oil. Add garlic, onion, celery, leeks, oregano, parsley and squid. Cover and cook gently for 10 minutes, stirring once or twice. Add tomato purée, stock or water, wine, undrained tomatoes, mushrooms, fish, and salt and pepper to taste. Bring to the boil, then cover and simmer gently for 15 minutes. Ensure fish is cooked through (it will be opaque all the way through, and will flake easily). Garnish with lemon slices and parsley. Serve immediately.

Honey Sesame Prawns (top) and Steamed Fish in Ginger (right).

Meat Dishes

Pork with Black Bean Sauce

PREPARATION TIME: 40 minutes

COOKING TIME: 45 minutes

SERVES: 4 people

225g (8oz) lean pork, cut into 2.5cm (1″) cubes
15ml (1 tbsp) oil
1 red pepper, cored, seeds removed, and sliced

Sauce
3 tbsps black beans, rinsed in cold water and crushed with back of a spoon
30ml (2 tbsps) Chinese wine, or dry sherry
1 tsp grated ginger
30ml (2 tbsps) light soy sauce
3 cloves garlic, crushed
1 tbsp cornflour
150ml (¼ pint) water

Mix together black beans, wine, ginger, soy sauce and garlic. Blend cornflour with 30ml (2 tbsps) of water and add to mixture. Place pork in a bowl, and pour over sauce. Toss together well. Leave for at least 30 minutes. Heat wok, add oil and stir-fry red pepper for 3 minutes. Remove and set aside. Add pork, reserving marinade sauce. Stir-fry pork until browned well all over. Add marinade sauce and remaining water. Bring to the boil. Reduce heat, cover, and gently simmer for about 30 minutes, until pork is tender, stirring occasionally. Add more water if necessary. Just before serving, add red pepper and heat through. Serve with plain white rice.

Lamb Meatballs with Yogurt

PREPARATION TIME: 15 minutes

COOKING TIME: 30 minutes

SERVES: 4 people

450g (1lb) lean minced lamb
2 cloves garlic, crushed
1 small onion, peeled and grated
½ tsp chilli powder
1 tsp garam masala
1 tbsp chopped mint

30g (1oz) breadcrumbs
1 egg, lightly beaten
30ml (2 tbsps) oil
75ml (5 tbsps) plain yogurt
Small pinch of saffron strands, or ¼ tsp ground turmeric

30ml (2 tbsps) boiling water
Salt
Pepper

Garnish
Fresh coriander or mint

This page: Beef and Oyster Sauce.
Facing page: Lamb Meatballs with Yogurt (top) and Pork with Black Bean Sauce (bottom).

In a bowl, mix together minced lamb, garlic, onion, chilli powder, garam masala, mint and breadcrumbs. Add lightly beaten egg to bind ingredients together. Add salt and pepper to taste. Wet hands. Take a teaspoon of mixture, and roll between palms, forming small balls. Heat wok and add oil. Add meatballs, shake wok to make meatballs roll around, and fry until browned well all over. Add saffron or turmeric to 30ml (2 tbsps) boiling water. Leave for 5 minutes. Add water to yogurt, and stir in until evenly mixed. Reheat meatballs and serve on yogurt. Garnish with mint or fresh coriander. Serve with rice.

Beef and Oyster Sauce

PREPARATION TIME: 30 minutes

COOKING TIME: 20 minutes

SERVES: 4 people

450g (1lb) fillet or rump steak, sliced into thin strips
115g (4oz) bean sprouts
115g (4oz) button mushrooms
1 red pepper, cored, seeds removed, and chopped roughly
2 sticks celery, sliced diagonally
2 onions, peeled and quartered
30ml (2 tbsps) light soy sauce
30ml (2 tbsps) peanut or vegetable oil

Oyster Sauce
3 tbsps oyster sauce
1 chicken stock cube dissolved in 30ml (2 tbsps) boiling water
15ml (1 tbsp) dark soy sauce
15ml (1 tbsp) Chinese wine or dry sherry
1 tbsp cornflour
30ml (2 tbsps) cold water
Salt
Pepper

Place steak in a bowl and pour over 30ml (2 tbsps) light soy sauce. Toss together well and set aside for at least 30 minutes. Meanwhile, mix together oyster sauce, chicken stock, dark soy sauce and wine. Blend together cornflour and cold water, and set aside. Heat wok, and add oil. Add onion, celery, mushrooms and red pepper, and stir-fry for 5 minutes. Remove from wok and set aside. Reheat oil and, when hot, toss in steak. Brown well all over, then add sauce and fried vegetables. Add cornflour mixture and bring to the boil, tossing continuously. Add salt and pepper to taste. Finally, add bean sprouts and simmer gently for 3 minutes. Serve hot with noodles or rice.

Sweet and Sour Pork with Peppers

PREPARATION TIME: 1 hour 15 minutes

COOKING TIME: 30 minutes

SERVES: 4 people

450g (1lb) pork fillets, cut into 2.5cm (1") cubes
1 large green pepper, cored, seeds removed, and chopped roughly
1 large yellow or red pepper, cored, seeds removed, and chopped roughly
1 small can or jar of Chinese mixed pickle
1 large onion, peeled and chopped finely
300ml (½ pint) peanut oil

Batter
1 egg
5ml (1 tsp) peanut oil
4 tbsps cornflour
4 tbsps self-raising flour
Water

Marinade
15ml (1 tbsp) peanut oil
2.5ml (½ tsp) light soy sauce
10ml (2 tsps) Chinese wine, or 15ml (1 tbsp) dry sherry
1 tsp cornflour
1 tsp sugar
Pinch of salt
Pinch of pepper

Sauce
4 tbsps sugar
100ml (⅙ pint) wine vinegar
100ml (⅙ pint) water
1 tbsp tomato purée
Pinch of salt
1 tsp cornflour
Small pinch of red food colouring (if desired)

Mix together marinade ingredients. Pour over pork pieces and leave for about 1 hour, turning occasionally. Mix together batter ingredients, with enough water to form batter. Add pork. Heat peanut oil in wok. When hot, deep-fry pork pieces in small batches, so that they do not stick together. Remove when golden brown, using a slotted

spoon, and set aside. Continue until all battered pork pieces are cooked. Heat oil again and repeat process, cooking pork for 5 minutes to make batter nice and crisp. Keep warm. Carefully drain off all but 15ml (1 tbsp) of oil. Heat, and add onion, peppers and Chinese mixed pickle. Cover and cook for 3 minutes. Remove and set aside. Heat vinegar, water, sugar, tomato purée, red food colouring and salt. Slake cornflour with 15ml (1 tbsp) of water. Stir into sauce. Bring to the boil and cook for 3 minutes. Add pork and vegetables to sauce. Serve hot with rice.

Beef Worcestershire

PREPARATION TIME: 40 minutes

COOKING TIME: 20 minutes

SERVES: 4 people

450g (1lb) fillet or rump steak, cut into 4cm (1½") cubes
60g (2oz) wonton wrappers
150ml (¼ pint) oil for deep frying

Sauce
30ml (2 tbsps) Worcestershire sauce
15ml (1 tbsp) dark soy sauce
1 tbsp sugar
Pinch of salt
Pinch of pepper
½ tsp cornflour

Mix together ingredients for sauce, and pour over steak. Toss well. Leave for at least 30 minutes, turning occasionally. Meanwhile, heat oil in wok. Fold wonton wrappers in half diagonally and seal open corners with water and press

Beef Worcestershire (top right) and Sweet and Sour Pork with Peppers (right).

together. Deep fry a few wonton wrappers at a time until golden brown. Remove with a slotted spoon and drain on absorbent paper. Repeat until there are enough wonton wrappers to go around the edge of the serving dish. Carefully remove all but 30ml (2 tbsps) of oil from wok. Remove steak from sauce mixture and

reserve. Heat wok, and when oil is hot, add steak and stir-fry until well browned. Pour over sauce and bring to the boil. Reduce heat and simmer, stirring continuously. When sauce thickens, and will coat steak well, place in warm serving dish and garnish with wonton wrappers. Serve immediately with boiled rice.

Pork with Plum Sauce

PREPARATION TIME: 40 minutes

COOKING TIME: 30 minutes

SERVES: 4 people

450g (1lb) lean pork fillet, cut into
*   2.5cm (1") cubes*
1 tbsp cornflour

This page: Beef with Mango.

Facing page: Pork with Plum Sauce (top) and Stir-Fried Leeks and Lamb (bottom).

5ml (1 tsp) sesame oil
15ml (1 tbsp) light soy sauce
15ml (1 tbsp) sherry
1 tbsp brown sugar
½ tsp cinnamon
1 clove garlic, crushed
1 spring onion, sliced finely
30ml (2 tbsps) peanut oil
4 tbsps bottled plum sauce
60ml (4 tbsps) water
Salt
Pepper

Garnish
Spring onion flowers

Mix together cornflour, sesame oil, light soy sauce, sherry, brown sugar, cinnamon and salt. Pour over pork, and toss together. Leave for at least 30 minutes. Remove pork and reserve marinade. Heat wok and add peanut oil. Add pork, and stir-fry until golden brown all over. Add spring onion, plum sauce and water to wok, and mix together well. Bring to boil, cover, and simmer gently for 15 minutes, or until pork is tender, stirring occasionally. Add marinade, and bring to boil. Simmer gently for a further 5 minutes. Garnish with spring onion flowers. (To make these, cut spring onion into 5cm (2″) lengths. Carefully cut lengths into fine shreds, keeping one end intact, and then soak in cold water until curling.) Serve hot with boiled rice.

Guy's Curry (Hot)

PREPARATION TIME: 40 minutes

COOKING TIME:
2 hours 15 minutes

SERVES: 4 people

1kg (2lbs) steak, skirt or rump, cut into 1.5cm (½″) cubes
1½ cups coconut cream
1 onion, peeled and finely chopped
3 cloves garlic, chopped
2 tbsps sultanas
1 tbsp curry leaves
1 dsp cumin
1 dsp coriander
1 tbsp vindaloo curry paste (or milder curry paste if a curry less hot than vindaloo is desired)
1 carrot, grated
2 apples, chopped finely
1 banana, sliced finely
2 tomatoes, chopped finely
1 red pepper, cored, seeds removed, and chopped finely
6 small pieces lemon rind
2 tbsps desiccated coconut
1 dsp sugar
1 cup water
150ml (¼ pint) safflower or vegetable oil

Accompaniments
1 apple, chopped finely
1 banana, sliced
1 red pepper, cored, seeds removed, and chopped finely
1 carrot, grated
1 tomato, chopped finely
2 tbsps sultanas
2 tbsps desiccated coconut
Half a cucumber, sliced, in 2 tbsps natural yogurt

Prepare fruit and vegetables. Heat wok, add oil and heat until warm. Add onion and garlic, and fry until golden brown. Remove garlic, and discard. Add steak and stir-fry until well browned all over. Add sultanas and stir in well. Add curry leaves, stir in, and cook for 5 minutes. Add cumin and coriander and stir. Cook a further 5 minutes. Add curry paste and cook for 10 minutes. Add grated carrot, red pepper, apples, tomatoes, lemon rind and banana and mix in well. Add water. Cover and cook for 30 minutes. Stir in desiccated coconut and cook for a further 30 minutes. Add sugar and cook for another 20 minutes. Add more water as necessary. Add coconut cream and cook a further 20 minutes. Serve hot with boiled rice and accompaniments.

Stir-Fried Leeks and Lamb

PREPARATION TIME: 10 minutes

COOKING TIME: 30 minutes

SERVES: 4 people

450g (1lb) lamb, cut into 2.5cm (1″) cubes
450g (1lb) leeks, cut into 2.5cm (1″) slices
1 tsp rosemary
1 tsp redcurrant jelly
1 tbsp chopped mint
1 tsp basil
400g (14oz) can plum tomatoes
15ml (1 tbsp) oil
Salt
Pepper

Garnish
Fresh mint

Heat wok, and add oil. Add rosemary, basil and leeks, and stir-fry gently for 3 minutes. Remove from wok, and increase heat. Add lamb and stir-fry until well-browned all over. Return leeks to wok. Add undrained tomatoes, redcurrant jelly, mint, and salt and pepper to taste. Cover and simmer for 20 minutes, adding water if necessary. Serve hot, garnished with fresh mint.

Right: Guy's Curry (Hot).

Devilled Kidneys

PREPARATION TIME:
1 hour 15 minutes

COOKING TIME: 20 minutes

SERVES: 4 people

450g (1lb) veal kidneys
15ml (1 tbsp) Worcestershire sauce
15ml (1 tbsp) dark soy sauce
30g (1oz) butter
1 tsp cornflour
15ml (1 tbsp) water

Devilling Mixture
1 tsp salt
1 tsp sugar
½ tsp ground black pepper
½ tsp ground ginger
½ tsp dry mustard
¼ tsp curry powder

Garnish
Sprig of parsley

Skin the kidneys and cut in half lengthways. Mix the dry devilling mixture together, and coat kidneys well. Leave for at least 1 hour. Heat wok and melt butter. Brown the kidneys quickly in the hot butter. Add Worcestershire sauce and soy sauce, and bring to the boil. Cover and simmer for 15 minutes thickening with cornflour mixed with water if necessary. Garnish with parsley and serve with saffron rice.

Calves' Liver with Piquant Sauce

PREPARATION TIME: 10 minutes

COOKING TIME: 25 minutes

SERVES: 4 people

450g (1lb) calves' liver
1 onion, peeled and sliced
15ml (1 tbsp) oil
30g (1oz) butter
1 tbsp flour
300ml (½ pint) brown stock, or
    300ml (½ pint) hot water and
    1 beef stock cube
2 tbsps tomato, mango, or other fruit
    chutney
1 tbsp tomato purée
1 clove garlic, crushed
1 tsp made mustard, English style
Salt
Pepper

Garnish
Chopped parsley

Heat wok and add butter. When melted, stir in flour and cook until lightly browned. Remove from heat and gradually stir in stock. Return to heat and add tomato purée and garlic. Stir until boiling. Add mustard and salt and pepper to taste, and let simmer for 5 minutes. Add chutney and mix well. Remove from wok and set aside. Meanwhile, slice liver very thinly. Wash and drain on absorbent paper. Heat wok and add oil. When hot add onion. Fry gently over medium heat until just turning colour. Add slices of liver in a single layer, and fry for about 3 minutes on each side, depending on thickness of slices. The liver should be cooked through and still tender. Do not overcook. Add piquant sauce to wok and toss together. Sprinkle with chopped parsley. Serve immediately on boiled rice.

This page: Devilled Kidneys (top) and Calves' Liver with Piquant Sauce (bottom).

Facing page: Sweet and Sour Pork and Pineapple.

oil and pour in black bean mixture. Add steak and vegetables and mix well. Make seasoning sauce by mixing cornflour with remaining 15ml (1 tbsp) of light soy sauce, and adding 1 tsp of sugar. When well mixed, pour into wok and stir. Bring to the boil and cook for 3 minutes. Serve hot with rice.

Braised Pork with Spinach and Mushrooms

PREPARATION TIME: 20 minutes	
COOKING TIME: 30 minutes	
SERVES: 4 people	

450g (1lb) lean pork fillet, cut into
    thin strips
225g (8oz) spinach leaves, washed,
    hard stalks removed, and shredded
4 dried Chinese mushrooms, soaked
    in hot water for 20 minutes, stems
    discarded, and caps sliced finely
½ tsp ground nutmeg
30ml (2 tbsps) water
30ml (2 tbsps) peanut oil
1 onion, peeled and quartered
1 clove garlic, crushed
1 tbsp flour
Salt
Pepper

Heat wok, add 5ml (1 tsp) of oil, and roll it around to coat the surface. Put nutmeg and spinach in wok, and cook gently for 5 minutes. Remove from pan. Add remaining oil to wok and fry garlic and onion over gentle heat for 5 minutes. Remove from wok. Meanwhile, add a good pinch of salt and freshly-ground black pepper to the flour and toss in the pork, coating well. Fry pork until each piece is browned all over. Add water and mushrooms, and return onion mixture to wok. Cover and simmer gently for 10 minutes, stirring occasionally. Add spinach and salt and pepper to taste, and cook, uncovered, for 2 minutes. Serve hot with steamed rice.

Steak with Black Bean Sauce

PREPARATION TIME: 1 hour 15 minutes	
COOKING TIME: 20 minutes	
SERVES: 4 people	

225g (8oz) fillet or rump steak, thinly
    sliced
1 large onion, peeled and chopped
1 large green pepper, cored, seeds
    removed, and diced
3 cloves garlic, crushed
1 tsp grated root ginger
1 small can sliced bamboo shoots,
    drained
3 tsps black beans
30ml (2 tbsps) light soy sauce
60ml (4 tbsps) peanut oil
5ml (1 tsp) Chinese wine, or 10ml
    (2 tsps) dry sherry
3 tsps sugar
1 tsp cornflour
5ml (1 tsp) sesame oil
Pinch of bicarbonate of soda
Salt
Pepper

Put sliced steak into a bowl, and sprinkle over bicarbonate of soda.

Add 15ml (1 tbsp) of light soy sauce, 1 tsp of sugar, wine, sesame oil, salt and pepper, and leave to marinate for at least 1 hour. Heat wok and add 30ml (2 tbsps) peanut oil. When hot, add steak and fry quickly. Remove from heat, and remove steak. Set aside. Add onion, green pepper, bamboo shoots, and a pinch of salt to wok. Cover and cook for 3 minutes. Remove and set aside. Make black bean sauce by crushing black beans and mixing with garlic, ginger, 1 tsp of sugar and 15ml (1 tbsp) of peanut oil. Heat wok, add 15ml (1 tbsp) of

This page: Braised Pork with Spinach and Mushrooms (top) and Steak with Black Bean Sauce (bottom).

Facing page: Fillet Steak Chinese Style (top) and Lamb Curry (Mild) (bottom).

33

Happys' Curry

PREPARATION TIME: 20 minutes

COOKING TIME: 30 minutes

SERVES: 4 people

450 (1lb) skirt or rump steak, cut into
  2.5cm (1″) cubes
225g (8oz) potatoes, peeled and
  diced
2 onions, peeled and chopped very
  finely
3 cloves garlic, crushed
1 tsp grated root ginger
1 tsp ground turmeric
½ tsp chilli powder
1 tsp garam masala
½ tsp salt
300ml (½ pint) water
60ml (4 tbsps) peanut oil

Garnish
Fresh coriander

Heat wok and add oil. Add ginger,
garlic and onion, and fry gently for
5 minutes. Add turmeric, chilli
powder, garam masala and salt, and
fry for 30 seconds. Add steak, and
stir-fry until browned well all over.
Add potatoes and water, and bring
to the boil. Reduce heat, and cover.
Simmer gently until meat is tender
and potatoes are cooked. Garnish
with fresh coriander and serve with
rice if desired.

Pork with Chilli

PREPARATION TIME: 1 hour

COOKING TIME: 20 minutes

SERVES: 4 people

300g (10oz) lean pork fillet, cut into
  2.5cm (1″) cubes
1 green pepper, cored, seeds removed,
  and sliced
1 red chilli, seeds removed, and sliced
  finely
4 spring onions, chopped
1 clove garlic, crushed
1 tsp sugar
1 tsp cornflour
5ml (1 tsp) peanut oil
5ml (1 tsp) Chinese wine, or dry
  sherry
150ml (¼ pint) peanut oil, for deep
  frying

Sauce
1 tsp chilli powder
30ml (2 tbsps) dark soy sauce
5ml (1 tsp) Worcestershire sauce
½ tsp five-spice powder
Pinch of salt

Mix together garlic, sugar, 5ml
(1 tsp) peanut oil, wine and
cornflour, and pour over pork.
Cover and leave for at least 1 hour,
turning occasionally. Meanwhile,
combine ingredients for sauce in a
bowl. Mix well. Set aside. Heat oil
in wok until hot. Toss in pork
cubes, and cook until golden
brown and cooked through – about
10 minutes. Drain and set aside.
Carefully remove all but 15ml
(1 tbsp) of oil from wok. Heat oil
and add green pepper, chilli and
spring onions. Stir-fry for 2 minutes.
Add sauce and pork, and bring to
boil, stirring continuously. Adjust
seasoning. Serve immediately with
rice or noodles.

Beef with Mango

PREPARATION TIME: 20 minutes

COOKING TIME: 15 minutes

SERVES: 4 people

450g (1lb) fillet or rump steak, sliced
  thinly
1 can mangoes, drained, reserving
  60ml (4 tbsps) mango juice
1 tsp sugar
½ tsp salt
1 tsp cornflour
Pinch of pepper
2 tbsps mango chutney
1 tbsp plum sauce
15ml (1 tbsp) oil

Combine 30ml (2 tbsps) mango
juice, sugar, cornflour, salt and
pepper, and pour over steak. Toss
well and set aside for 15 minutes.
Mix remaining mango juice with
mango chutney and plum sauce,
and set aside. Chop finely half of
the mangoes and add to the sauce,
retaining enough slices for
decoration. Heat wok and add oil.
Stir-fry steak for 5 minutes, tossing
well, or until browned all over. Add
mango-plum sauce and cook for a
further 5 minutes. Decorate dish
with reserved mango slices. Serve
with rice.

Fillet Steak Chinese Style

PREPARATION TIME:
1 hour 15 minutes

COOKING TIME: 20 minutes

SERVES: 4 people

225g (8oz) fillet or rump steak, cut
  into 2.5cm (1″) pieces
1 can straw mushrooms, drained
2 spring onions, sliced diagonally into
  1.5cm (½″) pieces
2 cloves garlic, crushed
1 can baby sweetcorn, drained
½ tsp crushed ginger
1 tbsp oyster sauce
15ml (1 tbsp) light soy sauce
30ml (2 tbsps) dark soy sauce
2 tsps sugar
5ml (1 tsp) sesame oil
5ml (1 tsp) Chinese wine, or 10ml
  (2 tsps) dry sherry
1 tsp cornflour
60ml (4 tbsps) water
Pinch of bicarbonate of soda
45ml (3 tbsps) peanut oil
Salt
Pepper

Garnish
Spring onion flowers (cut spring
  onions into 5cm (2″) lengths.
  Carefully cut into fine shreds,
  keeping one end intact, and then
  soak in cold water until curling)

Put steak in a bowl and sprinkle
over bicarbonate of soda. Mix
together light soy sauce, sesame oil,
wine, half the sugar, half the
cornflour, and seasoning. Pour over
the steak and leave for at least an
hour, turning meat occasionally.
Meanwhile, make sauce by mixing
30ml (2 tbsps) of dark soy sauce,
remaining sugar and cornflour, and
water. Mix together and set aside.
Heat wok, add peanut oil and,
when hot, fry steak for 4 minutes.
Remove from wok and set aside.
Add garlic, spring onions, ginger,
mushrooms, baby sweetcorn, and
finally steak. Add oyster sauce, and
mix well. Then add sauce mixture
and bring to the boil. Cook for
3 minutes, stirring occasionally.
Serve hot with rice, garnished with
spring onion flowers.

Sweet and Sour Pork and Pineapple

PREPARATION TIME: 20 minutes

COOKING TIME: 45 minutes

SERVES: 4 people

450g (1lb) lean pork fillet, cut into
  2.5cm (1″) cubes
1 clove garlic, crushed
1 tsp grated root ginger
30ml (2 tbsps) light soy sauce
1 tbsp cornflour
30ml (2 tbsps) peanut oil
150ml (¼ pint) water
30ml (2 tbsps) white wine vinegar
2 tbsps tomato purée
1 tbsp sugar
1 can pineapple pieces, drained

Garnish
Fresh coriander

Place pork in bowl. Pour over light
soy sauce and toss together. Leave
for 15 minutes. Make sauce. Mix
together vinegar, tomato purée and
sugar, and set aside. Heat wok and
add oil. Remove pork from soy

**Pork with Chilli (right) and
Happys' Curry (below).**

sauce, and add soy sauce to sauce mixture. Toss pork in cornflour, coating well. When oil is hot, brown pork well all over. Remove from pan and reduce heat. Fry garlic and ginger for 30 seconds. Add water. Bring to the boil, then return pork to wok. Reduce heat; cover and simmer for 15 minutes, stirring occasionally. Add sauce mixture and pineapple, and simmer for a further 15 minutes. Garnish with coriander. Serve hot with rice or noodles.

Lamb Curry (Mild)

PREPARATION TIME: 45 minutes
COOKING TIME: 1 hour
SERVES: 4 people

1kg (2lb) leg of lamb
2 tbsps natural yogurt
15ml (1 tbsp) sesame oil
2 tsps garam masala
4 cloves garlic, crushed
1 tsp grated ginger
2 tsps curry powder
½ tsp ground black pepper
2 tbsps desiccated coconut
1 onion, peeled and sliced finely
1 tsp curry leaves
3 ripe tomatoes, chopped roughly
30g (1oz) sultanas
1 potato, peeled and chopped into
    1.5cm (½") cubes
1 tsp sambal oelek
3 cups lamb stock
15ml (1 tbsp) peanut oil
Salt
Pepper

Garnish
1 tbsp desiccated coconut

Cut lamb into 2.5cm (1") cubes. Put bones in pan, cover with water, and bring to the boil. Simmer for 10 minutes. Strain and discard bones. Mix together yogurt, sesame oil, garam masala, garlic, ginger, curry powder, pepper and sambal oelek. Add lamb and toss well. Leave to marinate for 30 minutes. Heat wok, and add peanut oil. Fry onion and curry leaves. When softened, increase heat and add lamb and marinade. Brown lamb well. Add lamb stock, potato, tomatoes, desiccated coconut, sultanas, and salt and pepper to taste. Bring to the boil. Reduce heat and cover, and cook gently for 20 minutes. Ensure potato is covered with liquid (add water if necessary). Remove cover, and cook for a further 15 minutes. Serve

hot, sprinkled with desiccated coconut. Serve with boiled rice and poppadums.

Pork Chow Mein

PREPARATION TIME: 20 minutes
COOKING TIME: 20 minutes
SERVES: 4 people

300g (10oz) egg noodles
450g (1lb) pork, sliced thinly
15ml (1 tbsp) Chinese wine, or dry
    sherry
1 tsp grated root ginger
1 leek, sliced
1 red pepper, cored, seeds removed,
    and cut into strips
1 stick celery, sliced diagonally
30g (1oz) peas
150ml (¼ pint) chicken or light stock
15ml (1 tbsp) light soy sauce
1 tsp sugar
1 tsp cornflour
15ml (1 tbsp) water
1 small can bamboo shoots, sliced
45ml (3 tbsps) oil
Salt
Pepper

Soak noodles in hot water for 8 minutes, or as directed. Rinse in cold water, and drain. Combine wine, soy sauce and sugar, and pour over pork. Toss together and set aside for at least 15 minutes. Heat wok and add oil. Add ginger, celery and leek, and stir-fry for 2 minutes. Add red pepper and bamboo shoots, and stir-fry for a further 2 minutes. Remove from wok. Increase heat, and add pork, reserving marinade. Stir-fry over high heat for 4 minutes. Return vegetables to wok. Add chicken stock gradually and stir well. Add peas and cook for 2 minutes. Blend cornflour with water. Mix into marinade sauce and stir well. Add noodles and sauce to wok and toss together, heating through as sauce thickens. Add salt and pepper to taste. Simmer for 3 minutes. Serve hot.

Pork Chow Mein (right).

add half peanut oil and heat gently. Stir-fry peanuts for 2-3 minutes. Remove from wok, and drain on absorbent paper. Crush chillies, shallots and garlic to a smooth paste or blend. Grind peanuts to fine powder. Heat remaining oil in wok over a medium heat. Fry chilli paste for 1-2 minutes. Add 175ml (6 fl oz) water. Bring to the boil. Add peanuts, brown sugar, lemon juice and salt to taste. Stir until sauce is thick – approximately 10 minutes. Put in bowl, and keep warm. Heat wok, and add oil. Stir-fry meat until well browned all over. Serve with peanut sauce and boiled rice.

Piquant Lambs' Livers

PREPARATION TIME: 15 minutes

COOKING TIME: 20 minutes

SERVES: 4 people

450g (1lb) lambs' livers, cut into thin
   strips
60g (2oz) butter or margarine
30ml (2 tbsps) wine vinegar
1 onion, peeled and sliced finely
75ml (5 tbsps) white wine
1 tbsp chopped parsley
1 tbsp flour
Salt
Pepper

Garnish
Chopped parsley

Combine flour with a good pinch of salt and freshly-ground black pepper. Toss in liver and coat well. Heat wok and add half the butter over gentle heat. Add onion and fry gently until transparent. Add vinegar and cook over high heat until vinegar has evaporated. Add remaining butter and when hot add liver. Stir-fry briskly for about 3 minutes. Add wine, parsley, and salt and pepper to taste. Bring to the boil and simmer for 5 minutes. Sprinkle with chopped parsley and serve with saffron rice.

Steak with Peanut Sauce

PREPARATION TIME: 45 minutes

COOKING TIME: 30 minutes

SERVES: 4 people

450g (1lb) fillet or rump steak, cut
   into 1.5cm (½") cubes
15ml (1 tbsp) oil

Marinade
½ tsp chilli powder
Juice of half a lemon
2 tsps brown sugar
½ tsp salt
1 tsp ground coriander
1 tsp ground cumin

Peanut Sauce
30ml (2 tbsps) peanut oil
60g (2oz) raw shelled peanuts

2 red chillies, seeds removed, and
   chopped (or 1 tsp chilli powder)
2 shallots, chopped
1 clove garlic, crushed
1 tsp brown sugar
Juice of half a lemon
Salt

Mix together marinade ingredients, and marinate steak for at least 30 minutes. Make sauce. Heat wok,

This page: Steak with Peanut Sauce (top) and Mee Goreng (bottom).

Facing page: Kidneys with Bacon (top) and Piquant Lambs' Livers (bottom).

Kidneys with Bacon

PREPARATION TIME: 20 minutes

COOKING TIME: 25 minutes

SERVES: 4 people

450g (1lb) lambs' kidneys
1 tbsp tomato chutney
8 rashers streaky bacon, diced
1 onion, peeled and quartered
3 cloves garlic, crushed
30ml (2 tbsps) oil
15ml (1 tbsp) light soy sauce
1 tbsp cornflour
45ml (3 tbsps) sherry
1 tbsp chopped parsley
30ml (2 tbsps) water
Salt
Pepper

Garnish
Sprig of parsley

Cut kidneys in half and remove hard core with a sharp knife or scissors. Cut a lattice design on back of kidneys. Pour over sherry, and set aside for 15 minutes. Heat wok and add oil. Add bacon, onion and garlic, and stir-fry for 5 minutes. Remove from wok. Add kidneys, reserving sherry, and fry for 3 minutes. Stir in tomato chutney. Add soy sauce and water to wok, and return bacon and onion mixture. Add salt and pepper to taste. Cover and simmer gently for 10 minutes. Meanwhile, blend cornflour with sherry marinade. Add parsley and cornflour mixture, and stir, cooking gently until sauce thickens. Garnish with parsley. Serve hot with rice.

Lamb with Cherries

PREPARATION TIME: 15 minutes

COOKING TIME:
1 hour 15 minutes

SERVES: 4 people

450g (1lb) boneless lamb from leg,
    cut into 2.5cm (1") cubes
60g (2oz) butter or margarine
1 onion, peeled and chopped finely
½ tsp turmeric
½ tsp cinnamon
½ tsp ground nutmeg
1 tsp brown sugar
1 can black cherries, pips removed
15ml (1 tbsp) lemon juice
1 tbsp arrowroot
150ml (¼ pint) water
Salt
Pepper

Heat half butter in wok. Add lamb and fry quickly to brown well all over. Remove from wok and set aside. Add remaining butter and onion and fry for 2 minutes. Add turmeric, cinnamon, nutmeg and brown sugar, and fry for a further 1 minute. Add salt and pepper to taste. Return lamb to wok and add water. Cover and gently simmer for 45 minutes to 1 hour, until lamb is tender. And undrained cherries. Blend arrowroot with lemon juice and stir into mixture. Bring to boil and simmer for 4 minutes or until sauce has thickened. Serve hot with rice.

Mee Goreng

PREPARATION TIME: 20 minutes

COOKING TIME: 15 minutes

SERVES: 4 people

225g (8oz) fine egg noodles
60ml (4 tbsps) peanut oil
1 onion, peeled and chopped finely
115g (4oz) pork, finely sliced
115g (4oz) prawns or shrimps, shelled
    and de-veined
2 cloves garlic, crushed
15ml (1 tbsp) light soy sauce
1 tsp sambal manis or sambal oelek
¼ cabbage, shredded
1 green chilli, seeds removed, and
    sliced
2 sticks celery, sliced
Salt
Pepper

Garnish
Sliced cucumber
Sliced spring onions

Soak noodles in hot water for 8 minutes, or boil until cooked. Rinse in cold water. Drain in a colander. Set aside. Heat wok and add oil. Stir-fry onion, garlic and chilli until onion starts to colour. Add sambal manis or sambal oelek. Add pork, celery, cabbage and salt and pepper, and stir-fry for 3 minutes. Add soy sauce, noodles and prawns, and toss mixture to heat through well. Place in a warm serving dish, surrounded with sliced cucumber and sprinkled with spring onions on top.

Five-Spice Beef with Broccoli

PREPARATION TIME: 15 minutes

COOKING TIME: 15 minutes

SERVES: 4 people

225g (8oz) fillet or rump steak
1 clove garlic, crushed
½ tsp finely grated ginger
½ tsp five-spice powder
115g (4oz) broccoli florets
Bunch of chives, snipped into 2.5cm
    (1") lengths
30ml (2 tbsps) peanut oil
½ tsp salt
15ml (1 tbsp) dark soy sauce
½ cup hot water
2 tsps cornflour, slaked in 15ml
    (1 tbsp) cold water

Cut steak into thin slices, then into narrow strips. Mix together with garlic, ginger, and five-spice powder. Heat wok, add 15ml (1 tbsp) of oil, and stir-fry broccoli for 8 minutes. Remove broccoli and add remaining oil. Add meat, and stir-fry for 3 minutes. Add broccoli, soy sauce, salt and water, and heat to simmering point. Mix cornflour with cold water, and pour into wok, stirring continuously until liquid thickens. Toss in chives, stir, and serve immediately with boiled rice.

**Lamb with Cherries (right),
Five-Spice Beef with
Broccoli (below right) and
Boiled Rice (bottom right).**

Beef with Pineapple and Peppers

PREPARATION TIME: 40 minutes
COOKING TIME: 15 minutes
SERVES: 4 people

450g (1lb) fillet or rump steak, sliced
   thinly
1 can pineapple slices, drained and
   chopped
1 green pepper, cored, seeds removed,
   and chopped roughly
1 red pepper, cored, seeds removed,
   and chopped roughly
2 cloves garlic, crushed
1 tsp chopped root ginger

1 onion, peeled and chopped roughly
30ml (2 tbsps) light soy sauce
1 tsp sugar
2 tsps cornflour
30ml (2 tbsps) water
15ml (1 tbsp) peanut oil

Sauce
1 tbsp plum sauce
15ml (1 tbsp) dark soy sauce
1 tsp sugar
5ml (1 tsp) sesame oil
1 tsp cornflour
60ml (4 tbsps) water
Salt
Pepper

Combine 30ml (2 tbsps) of light soy sauce with 1 tsp of sugar, 2 tsps of cornflour and 30ml (2 tbsps) of water. Mix well and pour over steak. Toss together well, and put aside for at least 30 minutes, turning occasionally. Heat wok and add peanut oil. Add ginger, garlic, onion and peppers, and stir-fry for 3 minutes. Remove from wok and set aside. Add extra oil if necessary and stir-fry beef, well separated, for 2 minutes. Remove from wok. Mix together all sauce ingredients in wok, and heat until sauce begins to thicken. Add vegetables, beef and pineapple, and toss together over a high heat until heated through. Serve with boiled rice.

This page: Beef with Pineapple and Peppers.

Facing page: Duck with Orange.

Meals with Poultry

Duck with Orange

PREPARATION TIME: 30 minutes

COOKING TIME: 50 minutes

SERVES: 4 people

1 small duck
15g (½ oz) butter or margarine
15ml (1 tbsp) oil
3 oranges
300ml (½ pint) light chicken stock
100ml (⅙ pint) red wine
2 tbsps redcurrant jelly
1 tsp arrowroot
15ml (1 tbsp) cold water
Salt
Pepper

Garnish
Watercress
Slivers of orange peel

Pare the rind of 2 oranges and cut into fine shreds. Blanch in hot water and set aside for garnish. Extract juice from 2 oranges. Cut peel and pith from 1 orange, and then slice into rounds, or cut flesh into sections if preferred. Wash duck and dry well with absorbent paper. Heat wok, and add oil and butter. When hot, add duck, and brown all over. Remove from wok and, using poultry shears or a chopper, cut duck in half lengthways, and then cut each half into 2.5cm (1″) strips. Return duck to wok, and add stock, red wine, redcurrant jelly, orange juice and rind, and salt and pepper to taste. Bring to boil, reduce heat, cover and simmer gently for 20 minutes. Add orange slices, and simmer a further 10 minutes, or until duck is cooked. If sauce needs to be thickened, mix arrowroot with cold water and add to sauce. Bring to the boil, and simmer for 3 minutes. Garnish with slivers of orange peel and watercress.

Chicken and Cashews

PREPARATION TIME: 15 minutes

COOKING TIME: 40 minutes

SERVES: 4 people

450g (1lb) chicken breasts, skinned, boned, and cut into shreds
4 tsps cornflour
15ml (1 tbsp) light soy sauce
60ml (4 tbsps) peanut oil
30ml (2 tbsps) water
1 stick celery, sliced thinly
½ cup roasted cashews
115g (4oz) green beans, trimmed and sliced
1 clove garlic, crushed
1 onion, peeled and sliced
1 carrot, cut into matchstick strips
2 spring onions, sliced
½ cup chicken stock, made from chicken bones, or ½ cup of hot water plus 1 chicken stock cube
½ tsp five-spice powder
Salt
Pepper

Simmer chicken bones in a little water to make chicken stock, or dissolve chicken stock cube in hot water. Set aside to cool. Combine half the cornflour, the five-spice powder, and a pinch of salt. Toss in chicken and mix well. Heat wok, add peanut oil and, when hot, add chicken pieces a few at a time, tossing well. Stir-fry until chicken just starts to change colour – about 3 minutes. Lift out with a slotted spoon, and drain on absorbent paper. Repeat until all chicken is done. Carefully pour off all but 15ml (1 tbsp) of oil. Add onion and garlic, and cook for 2 minutes. Add celery, beans, carrot, and spring onions, and stir-fry for 2 minutes. Add strained chicken stock, and cook for 3 minutes until vegetables are tender but still crisp. Slake remaining cornflour with 30ml (2 tbsps) of water. Add soy sauce, and pour into wok. Adjust seasoning if necessary. Bring back to the boil and let simmer for 3 minutes. Add chicken and heat through. Remove from heat. Stir in cashews, and serve at once with noodles or rice.

Chicken with Mango

PREPARATION TIME: 5 minutes

COOKING TIME: 30 minutes

SERVES: 4 people

4 chicken breasts, cut into shreds
2 ripe mangoes, sliced, or 1 can sliced
    mangoes, drained
4 spring onions, sliced diagonally
½ tsp ground cinnamon
1 tsp grated ginger
15ml (1 tbsp) light soy sauce
1 chicken stock cube
150ml (¼ pint) water
30ml (2 tbsps) oil
30ml (2 tbsps) sweet sherry
1 tsp sugar
Salt
Pepper

Heat wok and add oil. Add ginger and cinnamon, and fry for 30 seconds. Add chicken and spring onions, and stir-fry for 5 minutes. Add light soy sauce, crumbled chicken stock cube, water and sugar, and bring to boil. Add salt and pepper to taste, and simmer for 15 minutes. Add mangoes and sherry, and simmer, uncovered, until sauce has reduced and thickened. Serve hot with boiled rice.

Stir-Fried Chicken with Yellow Bean Paste

PREPARATION TIME:
1 hour 10 minutes

COOKING TIME: 20 minutes

SERVES: 4 people

450g (1lb) chicken breasts, sliced
    thinly
30ml (2 tbsps) oil
2 tbsps yellow bean paste
1 tsp sugar
1 egg white, lightly beaten
15ml (1 tbsp) rice vinegar
15ml (1 tbsp) light soy sauce
1 tbsp cornflour
Salt
Pepper

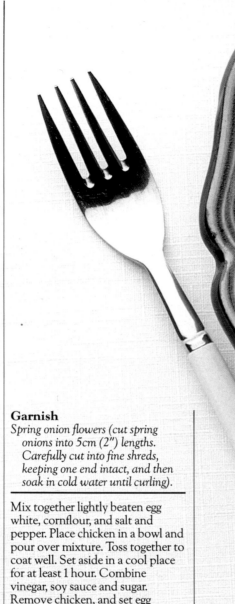

Garnish
Spring onion flowers (cut spring
    onions into 5cm (2") lengths.
    Carefully cut into fine shreds,
    keeping one end intact, and then
    soak in cold water until curling).

Mix together lightly beaten egg white, cornflour, and salt and pepper. Place chicken in a bowl and pour over mixture. Toss together to coat well. Set aside in a cool place for at least 1 hour. Combine vinegar, soy sauce and sugar. Remove chicken, and set egg mixture aside. Heat wok, and add oil. When hot, stir-fry chicken until lightly browned. Remove from wok. Add bean paste to wok and stir-fry for 1 minute. Add vinegar mixture and stir in well. Return chicken to pan, and fry gently for 2 minutes. Finally, add egg mixture, and simmer until sauce thickens, stirring all the time. Garnish with spring onion flowers. Serve immediately with boiled rice.

Soy Chicken Wings

PREPARATION TIME:
1 hour 10 minutes

COOKING TIME: 20 minutes

SERVES: 4 people

1kg (2lbs) chicken wings
½ tsp crushed root ginger
15ml (1 tbsp) Chinese wine, or 30ml
    (2 tbsps) dry sherry
15ml (1 tbsp) light soy sauce
15ml (1 tbsp) dark soy sauce
1 tbsp sugar
30ml (2 tbsps) peanut oil
1 tsp cornflour
10ml (2 tsps) sesame oil
1 star anise
2 spring onions, sliced
45ml (3 tbsps) water
Salt
Pepper

Wash chicken wings, and dry on absorbent paper. Mix together ginger, light soy sauce, sugar, cornflour, sesame oil, wine, and seasoning. Pour marinade over chicken wings and leave for at least 1 hour, turning occasionally. Heat peanut oil until very hot. Add spring onions and chicken wings,

Chicken with Mango (left) and Stir-Fried Chicken with Yellow Bean Paste (below).

and fry until chicken has browned well on all sides. Add dark soy sauce, star anise and water. Bring to the boil, and simmer for 15 minutes. Remove star anise. Serve hot or cold.

Chicken Livers with Peppers

PREPARATION TIME: 30 minutes

COOKING TIME: 15 minutes

SERVES: 4 people

450g (1lb) chicken livers
4 Chinese mushrooms
1 green pepper
1 red pepper
15ml (1 tbsp) rice vinegar
2 tsps sugar
30g (1oz) fresh ginger
1 small leek
45ml (3 tbsps) vegetable oil
1 onion

Garnish
2 spring onion flowers (trim and slice
  lengthways, keep one end intact,
  and leave in cold water in
  refrigerator until curling)

Soak mushrooms in hot water for 20 minutes. Clean and trim chicken livers, and blanch in boiling water for 3 minutes. Drain and slice. Peel

and finely slice ginger. Mix vinegar and sugar, and add ginger, and set aside. Clean and trim leek and cut into thin rings. Peel and slice onion and cut into strips. Core and remove seeds from peppers, and cut into strips. Drain mushrooms, remove hard stalks, and cut caps into thin slices. Heat wok, add oil,

and, when hot, add mushrooms, onion, leek and peppers, and stir-fry for 5 minutes. Remove and set aside. Add liver and ginger mixture. Stir-fry for a further 5 minutes, return vegetable mixture to wok and heat through. Serve garnished with spring onion flowers.

This page: Chicken with Cashews (top) and Soy Chicken Wings (bottom), and Chicken Livers with Peppers (right).

brown. Increase heat and add curry powder. Fry for 30 seconds. Add salt and vinegar, and cook for 1 minute. Add chicken, and turn so that mixture coats chicken well. Add coconut cream and milk, and simmer gently over a low heat for 20 minutes. Serve with boiled rice.

Honey Soy Chicken Wings

PREPARATION TIME: 5 minutes

COOKING TIME: 30 minutes

SERVES: 4 people

450g (1lb) chicken wings
½ tsp salt
30ml (2 tbsps) peanut oil
60ml (4 tbsps) light soy sauce
30ml (2 tbsps) clear honey
1 clove garlic, crushed
1 tsp ginger, freshly grated
1 tsp sesame seeds

Heat wok, add oil, and when hot, add chicken wings and fry for 10 minutes. Pour off excess oil carefully. Add soy sauce, honey, sesame seeds, garlic, grated ginger and salt. Reduce heat, and gently simmer for 20 minutes, turning occasionally. Serve hot or cold with rice.

Sesame Fried Chicken

PREPARATION TIME: 10 minutes

COOKING TIME: 30 minutes

SERVES: 4 people

450g (1lb) chicken breasts, or 4 good-sized pieces
115g (4oz) plain flour
1 tsp salt
1 tsp pepper
60g (2oz) sesame seeds
2 tsps paprika
1 egg, beaten, with 15ml (1 tbsp) water
45ml (3 tbsps) olive oil

Sift flour onto a sheet of grease-proof paper and stir in salt, pepper, paprika and sesame seeds. Dip chicken breasts in egg and water mixture, then coat well in seasoned

Chicken Curry (Mild)

PREPARATION TIME: 10 minutes

COOKING TIME: 40 minutes

SERVES: 4 people

1½kgs (3lbs) chicken
15ml (1 tbsp) peanut oil

1 onion, peeled and finely chopped
2 cloves garlic, crushed
½ tsp grated ginger
2 tsps curry powder
½ tsp salt
15ml (1 tbsp) vinegar
150ml (¼ pint) milk
150ml (¼ pint) coconut cream

Cut chicken into small pieces: breast-meat into 4 pieces, thigh-meat into 2 pieces, and wings separated at joints. Heat oil until hot. Reduce heat. Add onion, garlic and ginger and cook gently, stirring continuously. Cook for 10 minutes, or until onion is soft and a golden

This page: Chilli Sichuan Chicken (top) and Honey Soy Chicken Wings (bottom).

Facing page: Chicken Curry (Mild) (top) and Sesame Fried Chicken (bottom).

flour. Heat wok, add oil and, when hot, fry the chicken breasts until golden brown on both sides. Turn heat down, and cook gently for 10 minutes on each side. Serve hot with rice.

Lemon Chicken

PREPARATION TIME: 5 minutes

COOKING TIME: 40 minutes

SERVES: 4 people

1kg (2lbs) chicken pieces
90ml (6 tbsps) oil

Lemon Sauce
Juice of 1 lemon
75ml (5 tbsps) water
1 tbsp cornflour
30ml (2 tbsps) sweet sherry
Pinch of sugar, if desired

Garnish
Lemon slices

Heat wok and add oil. When hot, add chicken pieces and toss in oil until well browned. Reduce heat and cover. Simmer for 30 minutes until chicken is cooked. Remove with a slotted spoon and drain on absorbent paper. Place chicken pieces in a serving dish and keep warm. Meanwhile, carefully drain oil from wok. Slake cornflour in 30ml (2 tbsps) of water. Put lemon juice and remaining water in wok, and bring to the boil. Add cornflour, and stir until boiling. Simmer for 2 minutes until thickened. Add sherry and sugar, and simmer a further 2 minutes. Pour over chicken pieces and garnish with lemon slices. Serve with boiled rice.

Chilli Sichuan Chicken

PREPARATION TIME: 40 minutes

COOKING TIME: 20 minutes

SERVES: 4 people

4 chicken breasts, sliced thinly
1 clove garlic, crushed
1 green pepper, cored, seeds removed, and diced
1 red pepper, cored, seeds removed, and diced
1 red chilli, seeds removed, and sliced finely
1 green chilli, seeds removed, and sliced finely
1 tsp chilli sauce
15ml (1 tbsp) light soy sauce
5ml (1 tsp) Chinese wine, or dry sherry
½ tsp cornflour
Salt
Pepper
150ml (¼ pint) peanut oil, for deep frying

Sauce
300ml (½ pint) chicken stock
2 tsps cornflour
5ml (1 tsp) Chinese wine, or dry sherry

Mix together 5ml (1 tsp) wine, ½ tsp cornflour, light soy sauce, and a pinch of salt and pepper. Pour over chicken and mix well. Leave to marinate for at least 30 minutes. Heat oil for deep frying in wok. When hot, toss in sliced chicken and fry until just colouring and cooked through. Drain well. Carefully remove all but 15ml (1 tbsp) of oil from wok. Heat, and when hot, add garlic, green and red peppers, green and red chillies, and chilli sauce. Fry gently for 2 minutes. Stir 30ml (2 tbsps) of chicken stock into cornflour, then pour remaining chicken stock and wine into wok. Add cornflour mixture and stir well, until sauce boils and thickens. Add chicken, and toss until heated through. Serve with rice.

Chicken Cacciatore

PREPARATION TIME: 15 minutes

COOKING TIME: 30 minutes

SERVES: 4 people

450g (1lb) chicken breasts, cut into bite-sized pieces
400g (14oz) can plum tomatoes
1 onion, peeled and sliced
1 green pepper, cored, seeds removed, and sliced
115g (4oz) mushrooms, sliced
2 cloves garlic, crushed
1 tsp basil
1 tsp oregano
1 bay leaf
2 tsps tomato purée
150ml (¼ pint) dry white wine
45ml (3 tbsps) olive oil
Salt
Pepper

Garnish
Parsley

Heat wok and add 15ml (1 tbsp) oil. When hot, add chicken and stir-fry until chicken is opaque – about 8 minutes. Add more oil if necessary. Remove with slotted spoon and set aside. Heat remaining oil, and add basil, oregano and bay leaf, and fry for 1 minute. Add onion and garlic, and stir-fry until onion is soft but not coloured. Add green pepper and mushrooms, and fry for a further 3 minutes. Add undrained tomatoes, tomato purée, wine, and salt and pepper to taste. Cook uncovered for 10 minutes. Return chicken to pan, and stir until heated through. Garnish with parsley and serve with spaghetti.

Chicken Cacciatore (left) and Lemon Chicken (below).

Vegetables, Chutney and Sauces

Sweet and Sour Cabbage

PREPARATION TIME: 5 minutes

COOKING TIME: 20 minutes

SERVES: 4 people as a vegetable

Half a small cabbage
30g (1oz) butter or margarine
45ml (3 tbsps) vinegar
2 tbsps sugar
45ml (3 tbsps) water
Salt
Pepper

Slice cabbage into shreds. Melt butter in wok. Put cabbage into wok with other ingredients and set over a moderate heat. Stir until hot, then cover and simmer for 15 minutes. Adjust seasoning if necessary. Serve hot. Good with sausages and mashed potato.

Gado Gado

PREPARATION TIME: 20 minutes

COOKING TIME: 30 minutes

SERVES: 4 people as a vegetable

115g (4oz) bean-sprouts
115g (4oz) Chinese cabbage, shredded
115g (4oz) green beans, trimmed
Half a cucumber, cut into batons
1 carrot, peeled and cut into thin strips
1 potato, peeled and cut into thin strips
15ml (1 tbsp) peanut oil

Peanut Sauce
30ml (2 tbsps) peanut oil
60g (2oz) raw shelled peanuts
2 red chillies, seeds removed, and chopped finely, or 1 tsp chilli powder
2 shallots, peeled and chopped finely
1 clove garlic, crushed
1 tsp brown sugar
Juice of half a lemon
100ml (⅙ pint) coconut milk
150ml (¼ pint) water
Salt

Garnish
Sliced hard-boiled eggs
Sliced cucumber

Heat wok and add 15ml (1 tbsp)

peanut oil. When hot, toss in carrot and potato. Stir-fry for 2 minutes and add green beans and cabbage. Cook for a further 3 minutes. Add bean-sprouts and cucumber, and stir-fry for 2 minutes. Place in a serving dish.

Make peanut sauce. Heat wok, add 30ml (2 tbsps) peanut oil, and fry peanuts for 2-3 minutes. Remove and drain on absorbent paper. Blend or pound chillies, shallots and garlic to a smooth paste. Grind or blend peanuts to a powder. Heat

This page: Gado Gado with Peanut Sauce.

Facing page: Stir-Fried Vegetable Medley (top) and Sweet and Sour Cabbage (bottom).

and sugar in wok. Bring to boil, and simmer, uncovered, for 10 minutes. Add mango and sultanas, and simmer gently until sauce is thick. Serve cool as an accompaniment to a curry.

Left: Sweet and Sour Sauce (top), Mango Sauce (centre) and Chilli Sauce (bottom). Tomato Chutney (right) and Mango Chutney (bottom).

oil and fry chilli paste for 2 minutes. Add water, and bring to the boil. Add peanuts, brown sugar, lemon juice, and salt to taste. Stir until sauce is thick – about 10 minutes – and add coconut milk. Garnish vegetable dish with slices of hard-boiled egg, and cucumber and serve with peanut sauce.

Sweet and Sour Sauce

PREPARATION TIME: 10 minutes

COOKING TIME: 10 minutes

Juice of 2 oranges
30ml (2 tbsps) lemon juice
30ml (2 tbsps) white wine vinegar
1 tbsp sugar
1 tbsp tomato purée
15ml (1 tbsp) light soy sauce
½ tsp salt
1 tbsp cornflour
30ml (2 tbsps) water
Pinch of red food dye if desired

Combine orange and lemon juice, sugar, vinegar, tomato purée, soy sauce, salt, and red dye (if desired). Place in wok and heat gently. Blend cornflour with water, and stir into sauce. Bring to boil and simmer for 3 minutes, stirring continuously. Good with fish, pork, wontons and spring rolls.

Mango Chutney

PREPARATION TIME: 5 minutes

COOKING TIME: 20 minutes

1 can mango slices, drained and
*   chopped*
1 cup white wine vinegar
2 cloves garlic, crushed
1 tsp chopped root ginger
½ tsp five-spice powder
1 tsp salt
60g (2oz) sugar
30g (1oz) sultanas
Pinch chilli powder (optional)

Place vinegar, salt, garlic, ginger, five-spice powder, chilli powder

Ginger Sauce

PREPARATION TIME: 5 minutes

COOKING TIME: 10 minutes

1 tbsp grated root ginger
30ml (2 tbsps) light soy sauce
15ml (1 tbsp) Chinese wine, or dry
    sherry
1 tsp sugar
1 tsp cornflour
30ml (2 tbsps) water
15ml (1 tbsp) oil

Heat wok, add oil and gently fry
ginger. Mix together soy sauce, wine
and sugar. Blend cornflour with
water, and add to soy/wine
mixture. Pour into wok and bring
to the boil. Simmer for 3 minutes,
stirring continuously. Strain
through sieve. Good with sea-food,
pork, beef and crab rolls.

Brinjal Bhartha

PREPARATION TIME: 20 minutes

COOKING TIME: 30 minutes

SERVES: 4 people as a vegetable

2 large aubergines, cut into 2·5cm
    (1") slices
45ml (3 tbsps) oil
150ml (¼ pint) water
1 onion, peeled and chopped finely
2 green chillies, seeds removed, and
    sliced very thinly
½ tsp ground cumin
Pinch of sugar
10ml (2 tsps) lemon juice
Salt

Slice aubergines and sprinkle with
salt. Set aside for 15 minutes. Rinse
off salt and dry with absorbent
paper. Heat wok and add 30ml
(2 tbsps) of oil. Fry aubergines in
hot oil, browning lightly on both
sides. When all oil has been
absorbed, add water. Cover and
simmer for 15 minutes, or until
aubergines are soft. Remove from
wok, and drain. Heat remaining oil
in wok. Add onion, ground cumin
and chillies, and cook gently for
5 minutes without colouring
onion. Meanwhile skin aubergines,
and push flesh through a sieve or
blend. Add onion mixture to
aubergines. Add sugar, lemon juice
and salt to taste.

Special Fried Rice

PREPARATION TIME: 15 minutes

COOKING TIME: 20 minutes

SERVES: 4 people

2 cups boiled rice
115g (4oz) prawns or shrimps, shelled
    and de-veined
225g (8oz) Chinese barbecued pork,
    or cooked ham, diced or cut into
    small pieces
115g (4oz) bean-sprouts
115g (4oz) frozen peas
2 spring onions, sliced diagonally
15ml (1 tbsp) light soy sauce
5ml (1 tsp) dark soy sauce
30ml (2 tbsps) peanut oil
Salt
Pepper

Pancake
2 eggs, beaten
Salt

Garnish
2 spring onion flowers (trim spring
    onions, slice lengthways, leaving
    one end intact and leave in cold
    water in refrigerator until curling).

Heat wok and add 15ml (1 tbsp) of
peanut oil. Roll oil around surface.
Make pancake by mixing beaten
eggs with a pinch of salt and 5ml

(1 tsp) of oil. Add egg mixture to
wok, and move wok back and forth
so that the mixture spreads over
the surface. When lightly browned
on the underside, turn over and

This page: **Special Fried Rice**
(top) and **Ginger Sauce**
(bottom).

Facing page: **Brinjal Bhartha**
(top) and **Okra and Tomatoes**
(bottom).

cook on other side. Set aside to cool. Heat remaining oil in wok. When hot, add spring onions and peas and cook, covered, for 2 minutes. With a slotted spoon, remove and set aside. Re-heat oil and add rice. Stir continuously over a low heat until rice is heated through. Add soy sauces and mix well. Add peas, spring onions, bean-sprouts, meat, prawns, and salt and pepper to taste. Mix thoroughly. Serve hot, garnished with pancake and spring onion flowers. The pancake may be sliced very finely and mixed in if desired.

Julienne of Vegetables

PREPARATION TIME: 20 minutes
COOKING TIME: 15 minutes
SERVES: 4 people as a vegetable

2 medium onions, peeled and cut into matchstick strips
2 carrots, scraped and cut into matchstick strips
1 parsnip, scraped and cut into matchstick strips
2 sticks celery, cut into matchstick strips
1 turnip, peeled and cut into matchstick strips
15ml (1 tbsp) oil
30ml (2 tbsps) water
15g (½oz) butter
Salt
Pepper

Prepare vegetables. Heat wok and add oil. Stir-fry vegetable strips over gentle heat for 5 minutes. Add water and salt to taste, and increase heat. Cook for a further 5 minutes over high heat. Drain any liquid from wok. Add butter and freshly-ground black pepper, and toss to coat well.

Mango Sauce

PREPARATION TIME: 5 minutes
COOKING TIME: 20 minutes

1 can sliced mangoes
150ml (¼ pint) malt vinegar
½ tsp garam masala
1 tsp grated root ginger
1 tbsp sugar
5ml (1 tsp) oil
Salt

Heat wok and add oil. Add garam masala and ginger, and cook for 1 minute. Add undrained mangoes, vinegar and sugar, and salt to taste. Simmer, uncovered, for 15 minutes. Blend and push through a sieve. Good with chicken, beef and spring rolls.

Stir-Fried Vegetable Medley

PREPARATION TIME: 20 minutes
COOKING TIME: 10 minutes
SERVES: 4 people as a vegetable

2 carrots, cut into flowers (slice strips out lengthways to produce flowers when cut across into rounds)
1 can baby sweetcorn, drained
2 cups broccoli florets (slit stems to ensure quick cooking)
1 onion, peeled and sliced in julienne strips
2 sticks celery, with tough strings removed, sliced diagonally in half-moon shapes
1 courgette, sliced diagonally
1 clove garlic, crushed
15ml (1 tbsp) light soy sauce
¼ tsp finely-grated ginger
30ml (2 tbsps) oil
Salt
Pepper

Prepare all ingredients before starting to cook. Heat wok and add oil. Add ginger, garlic, onion, carrots, broccoli and courgette, and toss in oil for 2-3 minutes. Add celery and baby sweetcorn, and toss 1-2 minutes longer. Season with soy sauce, and salt and pepper if desired. Add cornflour to thicken vegetable juices if necessary.

Ratatouille

PREPARATION TIME: 30 minutes
COOKING TIME: 30 minutes
SERVES: 4 people as a vegetable

1 aubergine, sliced into 2·5cm (1") slices
2 courgettes, sliced diagonally
4 tomatoes, chopped roughly
2 onions, peeled and quartered
1 red pepper, cored, seeds removed, and chopped roughly
1 green pepper, cored, seeds removed, and chopped roughly
3 cloves garlic, crushed
1 tsp dry basil
60ml (4 tbsps) olive oil
Salt
Pepper

Slice aubergine and sprinkle with salt. Leave for 20 minutes. Rinse in water, and dry on absorbent paper. Chop roughly. Heat wok and add oil. Add onions, garlic and basil. Cover and cook gently until onion is soft but not coloured. Add peppers, courgettes and aubergine. Cover and fry gently for 15 minutes stirring occasionally. Add tomatoes and salt and pepper to taste and cook covered for a further 10 minutes. Serve hot or chilled.

Tomato Chutney

PREPARATION TIME: 5 minutes
COOKING TIME: 15 minutes

4-6 ripe tomatoes, chopped roughly
1 cup white wine vinegar
½ tsp garam masala
1 tsp salt
30g (1oz) sugar
2 green chillies, seeds removed, and chopped finely
1 tsp chopped root ginger
Pinch chilli powder (optional)

Place tomatoes, vinegar, salt, garam masala, chilli powder, chillies, sugar and ginger in wok. Bring to boil, and simmer, uncovered, for 15 minutes or until thickened. Serve cool as an accompaniment to a curry.

Okra and Tomatoes

PREPARATION TIME: 15 minutes
COOKING TIME: 10 minutes
SERVES: 4 people as a vegetable

225g (8oz) okra, sliced into 1·5cm (½") pieces
1 onion, peeled and chopped
2 tomatoes, chopped
1 red chilli, seeds removed, and sliced finely
¼ tsp turmeric
¼ tsp chilli powder
½ tsp garam masala
15ml (1 tbsp) oil or ghee
150ml (¼ pint) water
Salt

Heat wok and add oil or ghee. When hot, add turmeric, chilli powder and garam masala, and fry for 30 seconds. Add onion, okra and red chilli, and stir-fry for 3 minutes. Add tomatoes, water, and salt to taste, and cook uncovered for 5 minutes or until sauce thickens.

Chilli Sauce

PREPARATION TIME: 5 minutes
COOKING TIME: 10 minutes

4 tbsps tomato purée
½ tsp chilli powder
30ml (2 tbsps) Chinese wine, or dry sherry
30ml (2 tbsps) white wine vinegar
150ml (¼ pint) water
1 tsp cornflour
2 cloves garlic, crushed
1 tsp grated root ginger
15ml (1 tbsp) dark soy sauce
15ml (1 tbsp) sesame oil

Ratatouille (right) and Julienne of Vegetables (bottom right).

Heat wok and add oil. When hot, add garlic and ginger and fry for 1 minute. Mix together tomato purée, chilli powder, wine, soy sauce and vinegar. Add to wok. Blend cornflour with 15ml (1 tbsp) of water and add to wok with remaining water. Bring to the boil and simmer for 3 minutes, stirring continuously. Good with sea-food, beef, vegetables and spring rolls.

Sweets

Bananas Cooked in Coconut Milk

PREPARATION TIME: 20 minutes

COOKING TIME: 20 minutes

SERVES: 4 people

4-6 large, ripe bananas, peeled and
　sliced diagonally into 3 or 4 pieces
1 tbsp brown sugar
115g (4oz) desiccated coconut
450ml (¾ pint) milk

Garnish
Desiccated coconut

Put sugar, coconut and milk into wok, and bring to simmering point. Turn off heat and allow to cool for 15 minutes. Push through sieve or a piece of muslin to squeeze out juices. Return to wok, and simmer for 10 minutes, or until creamy. Add bananas, and cook slowly until bananas are soft. Serve immediately sprinkled with desiccated coconut.

Steamed Custard

PREPARATION TIME: 10 minutes

COOKING TIME: 20 minutes

450ml (¾ pint) milk
30g (1oz) sugar
2 eggs, beaten
3 drops vanilla essence
Sprinkling of ground nutmeg or
　cinnamon

Place sugar and milk in wok. Heat gently until the milk reaches a low simmer and the sugar has dissolved. Remove from wok and leave to cool for 5 minutes. Meanwhile, wash wok and place steaming rack inside, with 4-5cm (1½"-2") of hot water. Return to heat and bring water to simmering point. Pour milk and sugar mixture over beaten eggs. Beat again, and add the vanilla essence, stirring well. Pour mixture into a heat-proof dish or metal moulds and sprinkle lightly with nutmeg or cinnamon. Place on rack and cover with greaseproof paper, so condensation does not drop into custard. Cover wok and steam for 10-15 minutes. To test if cooked, a knife inserted in centre will come out clean, and custard will be set and gelatinous. Cover and cool for 1 hour, then place in refrigerator until needed.

Bananas Flambés

PREPARATION TIME: 5 minutes

COOKING TIME: 10 minutes

SERVES: 4 people

4 firm, ripe bananas, peeled and cut
　in half lengthways
60g (2oz) unsalted butter
60g (2oz) brown sugar
45ml (3 tbsps) brandy
Juice of 2 oranges

Heat wok, and add half the butter. When hot, add bananas, rounded edge down, and fry until golden on underside. Add remaining butter, and carefully turn the bananas over, so their flat sides are in contact with the wok surface. Sprinkle with sugar, 15ml (1 tbsp) of brandy, and orange juice, and allow to simmer for 3 minutes. Heat remaining brandy, set alight, and pour over bananas. When flame is extinguished, serve immediately. (Flaming can be done in serving dish).

Sesame Toffee Apples

PREPARATION TIME: 45 minutes

COOKING TIME: 30 minutes

SERVES: 4 people

2 large, firm Granny Smith or
　Golden Delicious apples
1 tbsp flour

Batter
30g (1oz) plain flour
30g (1oz) cornflour
1 large egg
30ml (2 tbsps) water
1 tsp sesame oil

Oil for deep frying
90ml (6 tbsps) peanut oil
10ml (2 tsps) sesame oil
9 tbsps sugar
2 tbsps white sesame seeds

Peel, core and cut apples into 2.5cm (1") chunks. Toss in 1 tbsp of flour. Combine flour, cornflour, egg and sesame oil in a small bowl. Mix to a batter with water and leave for ½ hour. Place oil for deep frying in wok, and heat to a moderate temperature (180°C; 350°F). Put fruit in batter and coat well. Deep fry several pieces at a time until they are golden. Remove with slotted spoon and drain on kitchen paper. Repeat until all fruit is fried. Repeat process to fry fruit a second time for a couple of minutes. Remove with slotted spoon and drain. When fat has cooled, carefully drain and clean wok. Fill a bowl with cold water and ice cubes, and put on side. Put peanut and sesame oil and sugar into wok, and heat until sugar melts. When it begins to caramelise stir and add sesame seeds and then add all of fruit. Toss around gently to coat in caramel. Take out quickly, and drop into iced water a few at a time, to prevent sticking together. Serve at once. (This can also be made with sliced bananas).

Facing page: Bananas
Flambés (top) and Sesame
Toffee Apples (bottom).
Steamed Custard (right) and
Bananas Cooked in Coconut
Milk (below).

Glossary

Arrowroot. The starchy extract of the ground root of an American plant, used as a thickening agent for sauces.

Bamboo Shoots (family: *Gramineae*). A native of Asia, this is the spear-shaped core of the young bamboo plant. The more tender winter variety is preferable, and can be purchased pre-cooked and canned in water. It should be drained before use, and will keep well in a dish in the refrigerator for up to 10 days if covered with fresh water that is changed daily.

Bean Curd. This fresh, white, custard-like curd cake, high in protein and hence very nutritious, is made from ground soya beans and gypsum. It is also available dried, fried, and in a yellow variety which contains less water.

Bean Paste. There are many varieties of this soy bean based paste. Hot, with the addition of chillies, is hot and salty. Sweet, with the addition of garlic, tomato purée and spices, is hoi sin sauce. Yellow, made with crushed yellow soy beans, is salty.

Bean Sprouts (Bean Shoots). These are the young, crisp sprouts of the green mung bean, and sometimes the soy bean. Available canned and fresh, the latter being preferable, and will keep for 2-3 days if covered with clingfilm and kept in a cool place. They are inexpensive, and can also be grown successfully at home.

Black Beans, fermented. Used in sauce-making, these whole beans are fermented and preserved in salt and ginger, and then dried and sold in plastic bags, or canned in brine. To remove excess saltiness, they should be soaked in cold water for about 10 minutes. Drained, and then crushed and used, they impart a pungent flavour to the dish. Black bean sauce can be purchased ready-made.

Chillies. There are numerous varieties of chillies varying in size and strength of flavour. Commonly used in Eastern cooking are the red and green finger-like chillies, about 10cm (4″) long, and the tiny red and green birds'-eye chillies which are very hot. When preparing chillies, it is advisable to wear rubber gloves and avoid getting the oils near lips or eyes. The seeds, which are very hot, should be discarded unless a fiery dish is desired.

Chilli Powder. Dried fruit-pod of the capsicum plant in flaked or powdered form. It is very hot and spicy, and should be purchased only in small quantities.

Chinese Rice Wine. A strong wine made from glutinous rice. A good substitute is dry sherry if it is unobtainable.

Chives *Allium schoenoprasum.* Now available in most parts of the world, they have a subtle onion taste and bright green stems which are used, snipped, as a garnish for soup and other dishes.

Cinnamon *Cinnamomum zeylanicum.* Delicate, sweet spice which is the dried, aromatic bark of a type of laurel. Sri Lanka and the Seychelles both produce this spice, which can be purchased in bark, quill or powder form.

Clarified Butter–Ghee. This is ordinary butter cleared of its impurities. When ordinary butter is heated, the top surface is skimmed clean, and when the sediment constituting milk solids has settled to the bottom, the golden liquid that is poured off is now clarified. With a higher burning point than most other oils, it is ideal for stir-frying and sautéing. It is also ideal for sealing pâtés.

Cloves *Eugenia aromatica.* The dried, aromatic buds of a type of myrtle native to South East Asia. Used whole, or with the central bud ground into a powder. A spice with preserving properties, it is used in sweet and savoury dishes.

Coconut Milk. Liquid extracted from white flesh of coconut. Can be made with desiccated coconut by adding hot water or hot milk, the latter being creamier, and letting stand until cool, with coconut milk squeezed out and the pulp discarded. Canned coconut milk can be purchased, but is expensive.

Coriander *Coriandrum sativum.* Chinese parsley. The fresh leaves and seeds of this plant are used, and are available in most parts of the world. The leaves have a fresh, pungent flavour, and are often used to garnish fish and chicken dishes. The crushed seeds in powder form are an important ingredient in curries.

Cumin *Cuminum cyminum.* The pungent, hot and rather bitter-tasting dried fruit of a plant related to parsley. This spice is very popular, and is an important ingredient in curries. It can be used whole or ground, and is an essential ingredient in garam masala.

Curry *Chalcas koeniggi.* The leaves of this South West Asian plant are used fresh or dried, and are a basic curry ingredient.

Dried Mushrooms *Lentinus edodes*. Shiitake. Tree fungus found in the East on oak logs and shii trees. They are sold dried, and have to be reconstituted by soaking in hot water for about 20 minutes. Drain, cut away stems and discard, and slice or dice cap. They are expensive, but only a few are needed to impart their distinctive woody flavour to a dish.

Five-Spice Powder. The combination of ground star anise, Sichuan pepper, fennel seeds, cloves and cinnamon. This fragrant mixture is often used to marinate soy-braised or roasted meat or poultry.

Garam Masala. A mixture of ground, roasted spices, usually consisting of coriander, cinnamon, cumin, cloves, dill, fennel, ginger and pepper. A flavouring used in many Indian dishes, it can be bought ready-made.

Ghee. See Clarified Butter.

Ginger *Zingiber officinale*. The root-stem of this South East Asian plant can be purchased whole, sliced, or ground. The whole root can be peeled as needed, and used sliced, chopped or grated. It freezes well and can be used without thawing first.

Julienne Strips. Cut into equal matchstick strips. Size can vary according to length of cooking time.

Noodles: Egg, Rice, Cellophane. *Egg:* require little preparation at home as they are usually pre-cooked by steaming. *Rice:* common in Southern China and, as their name suggests, are made from rice. *Cellophane* – transparent: usually made from mung bean starch paste, and used often in soups.

Oils: Sesame, Peanut. *Sesame:* oil extracted from the seeds of the sesame plant. *Peanut* – groundnut: oil extracted from groundnuts.

Oregano *Origanum vulgare*. Available world-wide, its leaves are usually used dried.

Oyster Sauce. Thick brown sauce made from extract of oysters, and sold bottled. Often used in Chinese cooking, its rich, subtle taste lends to other ingredients, whether meat, vegetables, noodles or rice. Can be added to a sauce, or used as a dip.

Paprika *Capsicum tetragonum*. A type of dried pepper, paprika varies from mildly hot to mild and sweet, and rosy-brown to scarlet in appearance.

Rice: Basmati, Patna, White Glutinous. *Basmati:* narrow, long-grain rice; one of the finest and most expensive. Grown in the Himalayan foothills. It has a subtle flavour, and is firm and separate when cooked. Best to eat with Indian food. *Patna:* long-grain. This versatile rice is very popular and is grown world-wide. The grains are hulled and polished, and when cooked remain firm, fluffy and separate. Good to eat with Chinese food. *White Glutinous:* very popular in Chinese cooking, particularly in sweet dishes.

Rice Paper. A wafer made with paste of flour, salt and water and cooked between hot irons.

Rice Vinegar. Made from rice, this is a clear, mild vinegar. A good substitute is white wine vinegar.

Saffron *Crocus sativus*. The dried stigmas of the Autumnal Crocus, this aromatic spice imparts a slightly bitter flavour and a bright yellow colouring to food, especially rice, and is one of the world's most expensive spices.

Sambal Manis. A combination of chillies and spices, often used as an accompaniment to Indonesian food, or in cooking, is mild and slightly sweet.

Sambal Oelek. A combination of chillies and salt, used in cooking – particularly Indonesian dishes.

Slake. Mix with a small quantity of liquid before adding to a liquid for thickening.

Soy Sauce. Used extensively in Chinese cooking, this sauce is made from soy beans. There are two types: dark soy sauce is thicker and not as salty as light soy sauce and gives a brown hue to food; light soy sauce is thinner and saltier than dark soy sauce, and used often in cooking.

Star Anise *Illicium verum*. The dried fruit of an evergreen tree native to China. This is an 8-pointed, star-shaped, reddish-brown spice. It can be purchased in powder form or whole. It has a strong aniseed flavour and smell, and is used to flavour stewed and braised meat and poultry dishes. It is also one of the spices that go into five-spice powder.

Turmeric *Curcuma Longa*. The dried and ground root stems of one of the ginger family. A vivid yellow powder, it is a spice often used in curries.

Water Chestnuts. These nuts are sweet and crisp, and are sold pre-peeled and canned in water.

Wonton Wrappers – Skins. Very thin wrappers made from a mixture of wheat, egg and water. They are sold fresh, usually in 7.5cm (3″) squares, and freeze well.

Index

Bananas Cooked in Coconut Milk 60
Bananas Flambés 60
Beef and Oyster Sauce 24
Beef with Mango 34
Beef with Pineapple and Peppers 41
Beef Worcestershire 24
Braised Pork with Spinach and Mushrooms 32
Brinjal Bhartha 56
Calves' Liver with Piquant Sauce 30
Cheese Nibbles 10
Chicken and Asparagus Soup 8
Chicken and Cashews 43
Chicken Cacciatore 50
Chicken Curry (Mild) 48
Chicken Liver Pâté 10
Chicken Livers with Peppers 45
Chicken with Mango 44
Chilli Sauce 58
Chilli Sichuan Chicken 50
Chinese Combination Soup 6
Crab Rolls 14
Crispy Fish with Chilli 15
Curry Soup with Meatballs 8
Devilled Kidneys 30
Duck with Orange 43
Eggflower Soup 8
Fillet Steak Chinese Style 34
Five-Spice Beef with Broccoli 40

Fried Bananas 10
Gado Gado 52
Ginger Sauce 56
Ginger Scallops in Oyster Sauce 16
Guy's Curry (Hot) 28
Happys' Curry 34
Honey Sesame Prawns 20
Honey Soy Chicken Wings 48
Hot and Sour Soup 8
Julienne of Vegetables 58
Kidneys with Bacon 40
Lamb Curry (Mild) 36
Lamb Meatballs with Yogurt 22
Lamb with Cherries 40
Lemon Chicken 50
Mango Chutney 54
Mango Sauce 58
Mediterranean Fish Stew 20
Mee Goreng 40
Okra and Tomatoes 58
Piquant Lambs' Livers 38
Poppadums 10
Pork Chow Mein 36
Pork with Black Bean Sauce 22
Pork with Chilli 34
Pork with Plum Sauce 26
Prawn Crisps/Crackers (Krupuk) 10
Prawn Toast 14

Ratatouille 58
Rice Paper Prawn Parcels 14
Seafood Combination 18
Seafood Hot and Sour Soup 12
Sesame Fried Chicken 48
Sesame Toffee Apples 60
Singapore Fried Noodles 20
Soy Chicken Wings 44
Special Fried Rice 56
Spring Rolls 12
Squid with Broccoli and Cauliflower 16
Steak with Black Bean Sauce 32
Steak with Peanut Sauce 38
Steamed Custard 60
Steamed Fish in Ginger 20
Steamed Fish with Black Beans 16
Stir-Fried Chicken with Yellow Bean Paste 44
Stir-Fried Leeks and Lamb 28
Stir-Fried Prawns and Mangetout 18
Stir-Fried Vegetable Medley 58
Sweet and Sour Cabbage 52
Sweet and Sour Pork and Pineapple 34
Sweet and Sour Pork with Peppers 24
Sweet and Sour Sauce 54
Sweetcorn and Chicken Soup 14
Tomato Chutney 58
Wonton Soup 6